A POINT IN TIME

A POINT IN TIME

The Search for Redemption
in This Life and the Next

DAVID HOROWITZ

Since 1947
REGNERY
PUBLISHING, INC.
An Eagle Publishing Company • Washington, DC

Cataloging-in-Publication data on file with the Library of Congress

ISBN 978-1-59698-290-1

Published in the United States by
Regnery Publishing, Inc.
One Massachusetts Avenue, NW
Washington, DC 20001
www.regnery.com

Manufactured in the United States of America

10 9 8 7 6 5 4 3 2

Books are available in quantity for promotional or premium use. Write to Director of Special Sales, Regnery Publishing, Inc., One Massachusetts Avenue NW, Washington, DC 20001, for information on discounts and terms or call (202) 216-0600.

Distributed to the trade by:
Perseus Distribution
387 Park Avenue South
New York, NY 10016

For Sarah

We miss you

Where do we go when we die? he said.
I don't know, the man said. Where are we now?

—Cormac McCarthy

David Horowitz is so powerful a polemicist that it is often forgotten how beautifully he writes. For the same reason, the deeply considered philosophical perspective and the wide-ranging erudition underlying his political passions are just as often overlooked. But it is precisely these qualities that come to the fore and shine through so brilliantly in the linked meditations that make up *A Point in Time*. With Marcus Aurelius, Ecclesiastes, and Dostoevsky as its guides, this little book boldly ventures into an exploration of first things and last that is as moving as it is profound.

—Norman Podhoretz

A beautiful book, both sad and uplifting. Moving in turns from the intimate to the universal, Horowitz not only explores but also embodies the dignity of the tragic worldview. *A Point in Time* is a poignant and elegiac reflection on life from a man who bears the burden of unknowing with courage and grace.

—Andrew Klavan, author of
True Crime and *Empire of Lies*

Emulating Marcus Aurelius, David Horowitz has produced a meditation on facing death that is poignant and wise. Whether invoking the Stoics or reflecting on his own father, he helps us think through that most basic of all questions: what is it that can give meaning to our existence?

—Walter Isaacson, author of *Einstein*

The voices of Dostoevsky and Marcus Aurelius resound through this profound, intimate, deeply moving and beautifully written meditation on life's ultimate questions.

—Gary Saul Morson, Prof. of the Arts and Humanities
Northwestern U., ed., Dostoevsky, *A Writer's Diary*

In this gentle and meditative memoir David Horowitz reflects on death and mortality, on loss and suffering, and looks for the ways in which consolation is available to us, and how it will never come from those schemes to remake the world and its human cargo that have wrought so much destruction in modern times. Horowitz is a skillful writer and a compassionate man, who has come to the other side of the righteous anger that he has directed at the great illusions of his generation, and discovered in himself the sources of peace. He has written a book of wisdom that will bring consolation to many who sympathize with his life-long search for order in a destructive world.

—Roger Scruton, philosopher

Why are we here? Is our journey an exercise in futility? Can our flawed nature be perfected in the here and now, or redeemed in a hereafter both impossible to know and impossible not to covet? *A Point In Time* is a gripping meditation on the central questions of any age by one of the truly great writers of our age.

—Andrew C. McCarthy, author of
The Grand Jihad and *Willful Blindness*

Marcus Aurelius, Dostoevsky, the family dogs, and Mozart mingle in these autumnal meditations. This is a deeply moving book about fatherhood and the faith of our fathers; the "rolling of souls" from generation to generation and the fictions we cannot wholly believe or wholly escape. Horowitz weaves his intimations of mortality with his indignation over the folly of those who think political artifice can repair the human condition. A profoundly personal and generous book, *A Point in Time* reaches well beyond its actual brevity. A copy of the *Consolations of Philosophy* under one arm, Horowitz takes us on a sunlit walk through the hills just as the shadows begin to gather.

—**Peter Wood, author of *Diversity***
president, National Association of Scholars

A pugnacious man in public, David has turned the arguments of his life into a gentle but firm meditation on the great moral issue of our time: the role of hope in history. He is also a learned man and learning has always come easy to him. But his knowledge is now also quiet wisdom. We are fortunate to have it. *A Point in Time* follows from the wisdom books of the Jews, from Psalms, Proverbs, Song of Songs, Ecclesiastes and other sublime testaments of three millennia.

—**Marty Peretz, Editor-in-Chief Emeritus, *The New Republic***

I have admired David Horowitz for decades. He has taught me many important lessons. But never have I been so moved by his writing as I am by this brief and profound book.

—**Dennis Prager, author of *Why the Jews?***

TABLE OF CONTENTS

CHAPTER ONE

OCTOBER 2006

I

As the years recede, as inexorably they must, and my step begins to falter, I have adopted a routine of taking my dogs for a walk up the long and leafy grade in front of my house, and back. It is the way I keep my body moving and my heart in shape, and how I fix an eye on my animal self, which unlike my imagination that could go on forever, will not.

There are four of us to keep each other company on these repetitive rounds—myself, two spirited Chihuahuas named Jake and Lucy, and a lumbering Bernese

Mountain Dog whom my wife has named Winnie after the fictional bear. The big dog's colors are black and brown with a white slash at the throat, and she limps affably behind us, hobbled by hips displaced from over-breeding, bearing it all without complaint.

As we make our way up the incline, the little ones race ahead spinning out their spooled leashes, weaving as they go like furry kites, their noses to the ground following invisible trails. Jake is a black and white spot who hurries nervously on spindly legs that narrow sharply at the joints creating a pink translucence where the light pokes through. Lucy, a muscular auburn, is the alpha of our pack, with moves aggressive and hunter-like. This martial presence, however, is undermined by ears that flop at the ends and quizzical brown eyes whose rims are wrinkled like the progeria children who grow old before they grow up.

Our point of departure at the bottom of the hill is a stucco house with sand-colored walls and a red tile roof. In the front a realtor's shingle indicates that my wife April and I have put the property up for sale. It is the third house we have lived in during a dozen years of a shared life. Our previous home in Malibu was perched like an eyrie on a cliff above the ocean, while this one is inland, overlooking the San Fernando Valley from hills above Calabasas. The realtor has attached a brochure to the "For Sale" sign, which promotes the property as a "Tuscan Villa," perhaps because it is set in a glade of the coastal range, or maybe because of the lion-head fountain on the garden wall. The interior is fitted with other details intended to lend it an Old Country look— a wrought-iron chandelier and a built-in ivory-colored cabinet whose surface has been distressed to give the appearance of age. Of all the environments I have lived in during the course of a life now reasonably long, this one has been especially comforting, and I am reluctant to leave it.

Our excursions begin with a procession to the end of the foyer where I have stored the dogs' leashes in a wicker basket and stuffed the brimmed cap I wear now to shade the sun-damaged skin that can no longer repair itself. I have only to reach for the hat to elicit a fanfare of yelps that celebrate the simple, evanescent pleasure before us as the high point of the day. And every day. For it is always the same.

I don the cap sparking their canine cries, and fasten the leashes to their collars, a task made challenging by the canine frenzy. When the tussle is concluded and the small dogs harnessed, we step through the front door to begin our adventure. The dogs charge at the squirrels and hares foraging on the lawn, causing them to scurry into the meadow by the side of the house or up the embankment across the way where they disappear into labyrinthine burrows and make good their escapes. A pipe corral rises above the warrens, which is home to a sable-coated stallion with a diamond emblazoned on his regal forehead. His name is Clifton and every day as we approach he subjects us to the same deliberate inspection. Nearby, his companion, an aged pony named Robin, stands so still he seems frozen in time. His matted hair hangs like a Spanish Moss from his weathered frame and makes him look so ancient I am always relieved to see him still with us.

And every day, without fail, we attack them. It is Lucy who sounds our battle cry, while Jake seconds her alarms prudently from the rear. Jutting her head through the bars of the corral, she finally provokes the majestic creature who turns and thunders towards us. The sight is fearsome to everyone but the instigator who elevates her cries at the stallion's approach, thrusting her body towards him. When Clifton is just above us, I yank her back. This precaution is not simply for her. Once when I failed to do so, she coiled on her tiny haunches and waited for the noble head to dip, then leapt and airborne bit the stallion on his cheek.

Inside the house, the little dogs do not lead as they do on our walks, but follow at my heels wherever I go. Whether I am ascending the stairs or descending, whether entering a room or leaving, their patter, like Marvell's chariot, is always hurrying near. I am the keeper of secrets whose mystery they seem to covet. *What to do? Where to go?* Is it an anthropomorphic folly that I am projecting onto these creatures? Perhaps it is. But such a skepticism also slights their need as kindred souls to keep their master close.

When the battle at Clifton's corral is over, we proceed up the grade to where other diversions await. Approaching a neighbor's yard, Lucy is again ready to summon its residents to arms. Behind these fences are less formidable foes but they still outsize us by daunting margins. Sometimes if our adversaries are inside the houses, or reluctant to leave the shaded overhangs where they nap, we will wait vainly for our challenge to be answered. But if they do come, a feral fury awaits.

Up and down the length of the fences the antagonists race snout to snout, teeth bared, jowls aquiver. I watch these skirmishes with a worried eye, since a slip too close to an opening would expose my reckless charge to jaws ready to decapitate. An occasional passerby displays alarm, but it is a misplaced emotion for the battles are not real. They are martial dances not unlike the ones that engage us in our ordinary lives, which also feature danger and mortality peering about the edges at each turn.

A furrow of autumn wind spins the leaves and unsettles the dogs with intimations of the oncoming weather. The season will indeed grow harsher but in the end will hardly seem a winter in this desert clime. This muffling of nature's cycles creates a sentimental fallacy for our aimless routines, no dramatic change of course, no auguring of brighter worlds to come. Having spent a lifetime avoiding occupations that appear to accomplish nothing, I find myself happy with this arrangement. It teaches me to embrace my circular horizon and accept it.

I am always impressed at how the dogs, familiar with every sight and smell along our way, come at these walks with renewed enthusiasm each time we set out.

As though life were an endless horizon always met for the first time. How their excitement when I put on my cap at the onset of our rituals never fades. How they do not contend with their fates but devour them as if their days will go on forever. But I, who do not have the luxury of their comity with nature, see the silence coming, and look on the brief turn of their lives with bittersweet regret, and mourn them before they are gone.

These walks are a peace I make with my own fate. Like my dogs, I look forward to a journey where the sights are familiar and nothing is accomplished, where nothing will happen that hasn't already happened before.

II

When I was still young and living in my father's house there were no dogs to take on our walks or celebrate our returns. It was not something I thought about at the time, or until long after I had animals of my own. But now that I have entered my own autumn and these dogs, with their quirks and affections, have become integral to my routines, the omission seems strange.

A recurring pattern of my father's days that he was never able to alter was the difficulties he had in his interactions with others. Social occasions would often end abruptly with him acting badly and feeling misunderstood. By contrast, he was able to approach animals with a confidence and ease that made the encounters pleasurable. Even as a youngster, I appreciated how the playful antics of the neighborhood canines never failed to amuse him; how, encountering them on our walks, his demeanor would change and a rare glow of happiness flush his sallow cheeks.

Whenever I have occasion to reflect on these moments, I am prompted to ask an obvious question. Why would a man who felt at odds with his fellows deny himself the pleasure of these loyal creatures, unlikely to be put off by his saturnine moods? Confronting this mystery, I am led to wonder whether his true desires were actually the secrets he was most determined to keep from himself.

Whenever the prospect of a pet came up for discussion, my father would camouflage his rejection as a practical matter. The responsibilities of caring for a creature who could not care for itself would distract us from missions that were more important. Or perhaps he was so firmly set in his ways that he was unable to imagine a life that was different.

This conservatism is an inertia that afflicts us all. We roll along tracks that have been laid down early in our journeys and are fearful of leaving them. So we rarely do. My own attitude towards these matters was an inherited disposition to which I hardly gave a second thought. When dogs did enter my life, it was unexpectedly, through the offices of others. It is only now that I have lived with them that they have come to seem indispensable, and that I can appreciate the gift I was given.

Much later it occurred to me that my father's inattention to primal needs was the other side of his passion for worlds that did not exist. My father was a missionary of the promised future in which a gentle rain of justice would nourish every seed. He never suspected that a fantasy so remote from the life directly in front of him might actually be the source of his isolation and gloom. By the time I was old enough to take my father's measure as a man, he was enveloped in a metaphysical despair so dense he could never break free. Black emotions weighed so heavily on him he could no longer read the books that lined his shelves, a paralysis that piled on even more regrets.

When I was alone in our house, which was often, I would sit on the blue-green living room carpet and study the shelves my mother had painted in a color to match. My parents had acquired almost all their library, fictions included, from a book club that catered to their progressive tastes. One by one, I would run my fingers over their spines and parse the titles on the faded jackets until I had memorized the placement of every text. Then I would pull them randomly from the spaces and slowly leaf through the secrets they held.

It was my mother who had acquired the membership, one of the many tasks she performed as the manager of our household affairs. An outgoing, curious, even adventurous woman, her tastes were catholic enough to provoke conflicts with my father when she favored an author who failed to conform to the party line. Her favorite books were not political tracts but biographies, usually of literary figures, and especially of the Russians—Tolstoy, Pushkin, and Gorky.

I can still see her propped on the pillows of her bed, holding the open volume of Gorky's *Mother*, which she read before going to sleep. When she had finished this text, she made her way through the six-volume memoirs of the Communist playwright Sean O'Casey, until she had completed the last one, *Sunset and Evening Star*. But her unlikely favorite was a social reactionary, the aesthete Marcel Proust, a French Jew who spent the last invalid decade of his life closeted in a Paris bedroom, retrieving memories of lost family and time.

Tucked away on the bottom shelf in my parents' library were a handful of dust-gatherers my father had kept from his college days, mementos of a philosophy course he had taken. I approached these volumes with a youthful reverence, viewing them as repositories of a proven wisdom I was expected to acquire. It is not clear to me now why I should have had such an attitude. The progressive light that infused our household threw dark shadows across the landscapes of the past, casting the ancients as child-like seekers in a primitive world, groping their way to fragments of knowledge through fogs of religious myth.

Among the relics in my father's unread trove was a volume bound in red covers, which featured a translucent page that veiled the photograph of a marble bust. It was the likeness of the Roman emperor who had written the book nearly two thousand years before. The *Meditations of Marcus Aurelius* was a text beyond my youthful ken, but if I had been able to comprehend it I would have seen that the counsels of this long dead author were a rebuke to everything my father believed.

What my father believed was that a time was coming when history would reward all the sufferings and trials of the past with a world in which human beings would live in harmony and be guided by justice and reason. Even though he was an atheist, my father's views were like those of a medieval Gnostic. He believed that the world was ruled by principles of darkness, and that knowledge was a light that would set men free. Consequently, when he read his morning paper it was not to gather tidings of events that actually affected him— prices rising, weather brewing, wars approaching—but to parse the script of a global drama that would one day bring history and its miseries to an end.

While my father's ambitions were grandiose, his actual footprints were so small as to be practically invisible. When he finally breathed his last breath, and we held a memorial for him in our living room, it was only attended by a small group of family friends. In contrast, the long dead author of the unread book commanded the attention of everyone alive in his time, while the thoughts he jotted down in his private hours are still read by us two millennia after he is gone.

Marcus Aurelius was the nineteenth ruler of Rome— the greatest empire the world had ever seen. But, unlike my father, he did not believe in history or human progress. The former he would have regarded as an illusion and the latter as nothing at all. This is what he wrote:

> *He who has seen present things has seen all, both everything that has taken place from all eternity and everything that will be for time without end ...*

III

Marcus Aurelius was born a hundred and twenty years after the birth of Jesus. He ascended the throne when he was forty years old, and commanded the Roman legions in their campaigns against the northern tribes. He was a warrior through eight winters before he finally succumbed to a fever in Pannonia, where he died in his fifty-eighth year. By all accounts he was an exceptionally good man. The English historian Edward Gibbon, chronicler of the empire's decline and fall, described the reign of Marcus Aurelius as golden—"a period in the history of the world during which the condition of the human race was most happy and prosperous."

Gibbon's comment may be regarded as a reflection of Plato's wish for philosopher kings who were both powerful and wise. But outside our dreams, no human age is golden, and the reign of Marcus Aurelius was no exception. His years on the throne were beset by familiar calamities: religious persecutions, plagues, famines, rebellions, and wars. Perhaps Gibbon accepted these sorrows as ordinary aspects of human unhappiness and chose to discount them.

It was said that in his later years Marcus was deceived by his wife, Faustina, who betrayed him in the arms of a Syrian governor named Avidius Cassius. When the emperor's failing health inspired premature rumors of his death, Avidius hatched a plot to seize the throne and proclaim it his own. Before he could act, however, Marcus learned of the design and returned to the capital intending to pardon the usurper and prevent him from doing himself more harm. But as soon as the conspirators realized what had happened, they turned on Avidius and slew him. Hoping to gain favor with the emperor, they brought the traitor's head to court as an offering to the intended victim. But Marcus scorned their gift as dishonorable and refused to see them.

When he died it was said of him that he looked on friend and foe alike with a compassionate heart. The evidence is the text he left behind in which no unkind word is recorded against his rival or his wife. His real name was Marcus Verus after his father who died young and his grandfather who raised him. "Of my grandfather Verus," he wrote, "I have learned to be gentle and meek, and to refrain from all anger and passion." And of his parents: "From the fame and memory of him that begot me I have learned both modesty and manliness, and from my mother I have learned to be religious, and bountiful; and to forbear not only to do evil but to intend evil." The Emperor Hadrian referred to him as "Verissimus"— more truthful than the name he had been given.

During the German wars Marcus Aurelius was bivouacked on the Danube River at Carnuntum. There, in his private hours, he secluded himself in his military tent and set down his intimate thoughts in Greek, calling the notes *Eis Ta Aon*, or "To Himself." The title *Meditations*, under which they found their way onto my father's shelf, was inserted centuries after his death by the monks who retrieved them, and who found in his writings intimations of their Christian faith.

I had read the *Meditations* as a younger man, but it was only when I re-read them in my sixties that I was finally able to see what he had written. By then, I was a decade older than the author when he departed this life; the volume with the red covers and translucent leaf was long gone, and my father was too. The copy I read was part of a set of more than twenty volumes in the "Great Books" series assembled by the *Encyclopedia Britannica*. The editors' idea was to provide readers with a shelf-long summary of the wisdom humanity had accumulated until then. The books belonged to my stepson, Jon, who was then in his teens, and had been given to him by his father, who never had the privilege of attending a university and wanted to give his son the opportunity he missed. In acting on this desire he disregarded (as all of us do) the biblical warning of Ecclesiastes: "In much

knowledge is much grief, and he that increaseth knowledge increaseth sorrow."

IV

Unlike my father, I do not look down my nose at the
ancients but am impressed by their understanding of our
case. How they were able to put a finger on the source of
our distress: that alone among creatures we know our
fate, and learn sooner or later that the world has no interest in it.

Marcus Aurelius was a Stoic, which is the name given
to a school of philosophy whose view of our dramas is
unfiltered by romance. To ease the heartache of our
human plight, the Stoics advised us to accept our lot and
refrain from contending against it. The counsel of the
unread book on my father's shelf was this: you cannot
alter the world, so do not make yourself miserable trying.

It was not simply a counsel of passivity in a situation
without hope. Even though you cannot change the world,
the Stoics observed, you can change what you make of it,
and thus how it affects you. Things outside us "do not
touch the soul, for they are external and immoveable,"

wrote Marcus Aurelius; "our perturbations come only from our opinion of them, which is within." Therefore look inward, for you are the emperor of your soul. There are no gains or losses, no victories or defeats but thinking makes them so. "Life is opinion." It is a story we write.

This being the case, it is wise to construct a narrative that does not multiply unnecessary defeats. Therefore, begin by regarding yourself as part of the natural world and not outside it. Other creatures also come into this life unbidden and leave no trace but do not complain. Emulate them. Make peace with your nature and you will be at peace with yourself.

If my father had read the Stoic's book, would he have been able to take this advice? Would its wisdom have helped to make his days less troubled? I have no reason to think so. By the time my father reached the middle of his journey, his mind was so freighted with feelings of failure that I do not think he would have been able to grasp that the failure is life itself, and there is no help for that.

V

Two hundred years after Marcus Aurelius's death, the crypt he was laid in was plundered by vandals so that not even his ashes remain. All that is left of his presence are the thoughts he set down, which live on to haunt us.

> *Look on times gone by. You will see people marrying, bringing up children; you will see them sick and dying, warring and feasting; doing business and cultivating the ground; you will see them flattering, putting on airs, suspecting, plotting, wishing for some to die, grumbling about the present, loving, heaping up treasure, desiring positions, power. Well, then, the life of these people is gone.*

Reading these melancholy words I am struck by the irony of our lives, how the nearer we approach the end of our journeys the less time is left to benefit from what we have learned; how the opportunities we were once offered appear in a light so different from when we could have taken advantage of them; how approaching the end of my days, I cannot imagine how my altered vision would have affected the decisions I made when I was just starting out; or whether knowing what I do now I would have been able to go forward at all.

VI

I was in my sixty-seventh year when I re-read the Roman's words, and could have been reading them for the first time. When I was young, every step forward seemed like the onset of a journey without end, and the morbid reflections of the Roman appeared like a distant commentary on the fates of strangers, unrelated to my own. But the years have worn through my defenses, and I am no longer stepping out on endless highways. Reading his observations now I can hardly regard them as references to a landscape alien and remote, but as a mirror of my own estate.

> *One man buries another and is laid out dead, and another buries him. Think how many physicians are gone after knitting their brows over the sick; how many astrologers after predicting with great pretensions the deaths of others; how many philosophers after endless discourses on death or immortality; how many heroes after killing thousands; how many tyrants who rule men's lives with terrible insolence as though they were immortal; how many cities dead and vanished …*

Think of the billions of strangers present in the world and the lives of which you have no inkling. How every one of them carries a world inside that is opaque to you, as though it never was. How that is exactly the way you are regarded by them. Well, then, what does your striving add up to and where is it headed?

> *Consider everyone you have known; how many things you have witnessed, which have already changed and how many people who have ceased to be. Observe how ephemeral and worthless human things are, and what was yesterday a little mucus, tomorrow will be a mummy or ashes.*
>
> *Be not troubled, for all things are according to nature and in a little while you will be no one and nowhere.*

Consider the emperor Marcus Aurelius and those who revered him, and how they have vanished. How only a handful of them left even the smallest mark, and how even that too will soon be gone. How a thousand-year celebrity is but a flutter in time, and is nothing at all to one who is unable to hear the echoes of his fame.

VII

Sometimes in the night, which is an image of this emptiness, I am haunted by reflections of death until I force myself awake to escape them. In the dark, which threatens to engulf me, I seek comfort in the familiar kiss of my wife's still sleeping flesh. Miraculously, I have only to touch her to bring myself back from the empty world to this. If she is settled in her dreams and I am reluctant to rouse her, I can reach for the small bodies curled like furry slippers at my feet who also provide me with a reprieve.

Sometimes I am roused by the banshee wails of coyotes shrilling over a kill in the canyon nearby. The unlucky prey may be a hare that has left its warren to venture into the night. But sometimes the shrieks are from a neighborhood dog that has strayed imprudently from his yard. These cries make me fearful for my companions, and I am oppressed by the terrible fate that awaits them should they leave their nest and wander abroad.

But the dogs sleep on beside me oblivious of the danger. Unlike us they do not dream they can live forever, or pretend to be something they are not. Nor do they expend energy attempting to persuade themselves they can be exceptions to a rule. They are scavengers of time, and consume their moments as they come. Consequently, they face their trials without protest, and are able to endure their suffering with a dignity that eludes us, and makes them perfect instructors in the Stoic idea.

Sometimes when I am unable to retreat into the caverns of unconsciousness, I wander in a purgatory of half sleep and fitful thoughts where I am harassed by images of our common fate. In this interregnum I am often overcome with remorse to think how I have brought four children into the world as hostages of time. And yet I have no more persistent fear than that of losing them.

VIII

Marcus Aurelius commanded an empire that spanned the known world, while his teacher, Epictetus, was a mere slave and master of nothing but his thoughts. Yet their shared destiny led them to a common conclusion:

"Make the best use of what is in your power and take the rest as it happens."

It was a practical wisdom they applied equally to the trials of history and the tribulations of an ordinary life. Every day, Marcus Aurelius advised, you will encounter people who are rude and deceitful. But do not rise to their offense or seek redress for the irritations they cause, for you cannot change them, and the attempt to do so is pointless. "Instead, ask yourself: 'Is it possible that shameless men should not be in the world? It is not possible. Do not, then, require what is impossible.'"

Useful advice if you can follow it. Consider how such an attitude can turn even the grave to advantage. Has someone wronged you? Observe how the event is already past and how time has begun to erase the circumstances of your hurt. Reflect on the fact that your tormentor will soon be gone. This is nature's way, to come and go. Let it go.

> *Often think of the rapidity with which things pass by and disappear, both the things that are and the things that are created. For substance is like a river in a continual flow, and there is hardly anything that stands still. Consider that*

which is near to you, this boundless abyss of the
past and of the future into which all things disap-
pear. How is one who is puffed up with earthly
things, or plagued about them, or makes himself
miserable over them, not a fool? For all these
things will vex him only for a short time.

In the Stoic world even the prospect of one's own dis-
appearance can seem a minimal inconvenience. A
Stoic reflects that the past is already gone and the
future yet to come; consequently, neither is yours to
lose. It does not really matter, therefore, how much
time you have left or how little, since all that can be
taken from you is the moment before you. Therefore,
it is of no importance whether you are destined to live
for one year or a hundred. For if someone were to tell
you that you will be dead tomorrow or the day after,
what difference would it make? "You would not care
much whether it was on the third day or the next; so
think it no great thing to die after as many years as
you can name."

These are the sober thoughts of the Roman, but of
what practical use? They do not tell you how one becomes

an emperor. Or how one gets through a single earthly day. Or why one should.

The philosopher is haunted by this ultimate question, and it is one that he cannot answer. "If the universe is only a confused mass of dispersing elements why should I desire to continue any longer in it? Why should I care for anything but how I return to earth again?"

Why indeed? It is the question toward which all Stoic meditations lead. Yet no answer follows. So he asks it again:

"If there are no gods, or if there are gods but they do not take care of the world, why should I desire to live in such a world?" And then again: "The universe is *either* a confusion and a dispersion, *or* it is an order and providence. If it is the former, why do I desire to remain any longer in a meaningless chaos, destined for oblivion?"

In his heart of hearts not even a Stoic can live with the thought that all his efforts are without meaning and that every trace of him will one day vanish. Nothing I encountered in the pages of the *Meditations* made as strong or as troubling an impression on me as these passages in which the philosopher wrestles with his dilemma and struggles vainly to extricate himself from it.

In the end, he decides to pose the question differently so that it will seem to answer itself: "Either this world is a chaos, or it is a work of beauty, and though seemingly trackless and confused, governed by a certain order."

In other words, our perception of beauty reveals the existence of order—a design within which our lives make sense. But why? Is appearance to be taken as truth? Why should the appearance of beauty be any different than the appearance of meaning? Even an atheist will feel as though his actions are meaningful. But does that mean they are? Do our lives make sense outside the stories we tell ourselves? Can they?

The answer the Roman finally offers is the familiar assertion of a religious faith: "There are certainly gods, and they take care of the world." And that is all he has to say. No evidence is provided for the newfound optimism that appears with these words and no apologies for the fact that it contradicts his previous advice. For if there are gods who care for us, why must we resign ourselves to a discouraging fate? Why is a Stoic wisdom necessary, and why does it direct us towards the path of acceptance and retreat? What sense can be made of those grim warnings: *In a little while you will be no one and will soon be nowhere?*

There are still shameless people in the world, but we are no longer invited to reconcile ourselves to what we cannot change. We are counseled instead to adopt a superior air knowing that there will be justice one day, even if now there appears to be none. "When you rise in the morning, say to yourself, I shall meet today intrusive, ungrateful, arrogant, deceitful, envious and uncharitable men. All these bad qualities in the people we encounter are theirs by reason of their ignorance of what is good and evil. But I who have seen the nature of the good that it is beautiful, and of the bad that it is ugly, and the nature of him who does wrong, that it is akin to me— that it is not only of the same blood or seed, but participates in the same intelligence and the same portion of the divinity—cannot be injured by any of them."

Gone is the Stoic voice to be replaced by the prophet's: "Constantly regard the universe as one living being, having one substance and one soul, for all things are linked and knitted together, and the knot is sacred. For all things there is but one and the same order, and through all things, one and the same God. For all things there is the same substance and the same law. There is one common reason, and one common truth: One perfection."

If a Stoic cannot live without gods who care for him, or a perfection that makes sense of our lives, who can? The philosopher who set out to describe how we ought to live inadvertently reveals how we do: by inhabiting stories that have no end.

Credo ergo sum. I believe, therefore I am.

IX

Because my father viewed history as a forward march, many authors were missing from his shelves, among them the Russian writer, Fyodor Dostoevsky, who began life as a radical but ended as an unrelenting critic of the romance that absorbed my father's days. As a result Dostoevsky was shunned by progressives like my father as a "social reactionary," an enemy of the future.

I am struck now by the irony of this parental attitude, which appears to me as an emblem of how irretrievably our lives remain beyond our control. For eventually I left the path on which my father hoped to find refuge from his unhappy life. No longer blinded by this utopian light, I discovered in the forbidden author insights that helped to wake me from the dreams that had stifled my father's life.

Fyodor Dostoevsky was born in Moscow's Hospital for the Poor in the year 1821, which by a quirk of the calendar was exactly seventeen centuries after the Roman's birth. A tic of our nature prompts us to seek significance in coincidences like this but there are none. No chronological links exist outside the stories we tell, and there are no comforting architectures in the movements of time. In the year 18211 or 182111 who will remark on the synchronicity of these celebrated births? However impressive to us, the seventeen centuries that separated them will mean nothing to someone born ten or twenty thousand years after we are gone. Who, then, will even read their books, or remember who they were?

Dostoevsky's father was a physician in residence in the Hospital for the Poor, and a person of means. He was also an alcoholic, a man of selfish desires and lecherous drives, who misused both his family and his serfs. When he died under circumstances that were murky and suspicious, his son concluded that he had been murdered by one of his victims seeking revenge. As a writer, Dostoevsky was obsessed with the problem of evil and the human will to pursue it. The killing of an abusive father by a resentful son and a rebellion against God are the dark centers of his greatest work, *The Brothers Karam-azov*, which he completed a few months before he died in his sixtieth year.

Dostoevsky had a previous brush with oblivion at the outset of his career. The chain of circumstances that led to it began when his first book was discovered by the literary critic, Vissarion Belinsky, whose praise helped him to gain fame as a young man still in his twenties. Belinsky was also a socialist and recruited him into a circle of St. Petersburg radicals who were planning a revolution in Russia. Four years after Dostoevsky joined the circle, its members were arrested on charges of plotting to kill the Czar. The accused were brought to trial and convicted, but their sentencing was postponed and they were held in the Peter and Paul Fortress, where they were kept in the dark about their eventual fate.

On a December morning in 1849, Dostoevsky and his cohorts were taken from their cells and led out into the streets of St. Petersburg, which were blanketed in a freshly fallen snow. The prisoners were marched to the Semyonovsky Parade Ground where a phalanx of soldiers awaited them. In the courtyard, three stakes had been planted, which stood out starkly in the winter light.

An arctic wind burned the prisoners' faces while an officer read their sentences aloud. For crimes against the state, the guilty were to be executed by firing squad, the sentences to be carried out at once in groups of three. Dostoevsky was assigned to the second group.

Years later, Dostoevsky described the scene in one of his novels: "The first three were led to the posts and tied to them, the death vestments (long white smocks) were put on them, and white caps were drawn over their eyes so that they shouldn't see the rifles.... The priest went to each of them with the cross."

The howling of the wind made it difficult for the prisoners to hear each man's name as it was read aloud, and then the order was given and the rifles loaded. The firing squad took aim, and everything grew still. Just before the first shot was to be fired, a white flag was raised and a soldier read aloud a royal reprieve. The entire drama had been contrived by the Czar to punish the rebel youth.

In his novel, Dostoevsky reported the feelings he had in the moments before his execution was to take place. These can be taken as a test of the Roman's idea that it should not matter whether our exit comes on this day or the next:

> *Those five minutes seemed to him an infinite time, a vast wealth; he felt that he had so many lives left that there was no need yet to think of the last moment, so much so that he divided his time up. He set aside time to take leave of his comrades, two minutes for that; then he kept another two minutes to think for the last time; and then a minute to look about him for the last time.... He was dying at twenty-seven, strong and healthy.... Nothing was so dreadful at that time as the continual thought, "What if I were not to die! What if I could go back to life—what eternity! And it would all be mine! I would turn every minute into an age; I would lose nothing. I would count every minute as it passed. I would not waste one!"*

Here Dostoevsky reveals that our last moments matter to us and cannot be separated from our hopes for the future. His response could be interpreted as the flush of a young man's illusion that he will go on forever, or the optimism of a Christian convinced that he is headed for a better world. But from a Stoic point of view it doesn't really matter which. Why should the condemned man savor his last moments *wherever* he is going? Why should he care about farewells? Why thirst for one more draught of a life already lost?

Dostoevsky's actual feelings in his last moments remind us of what the Roman forgot: the sensual pull of the tangible world; the hunger for the life we taste, as opposed to the one we merely think about. The desire for *this* life, regardless of how much we get of it.

X

After his reprieve by the Czar, the prisoner was exiled to a penal camp in Siberia to serve out a four-year sentence. His mock death and subsequent resurrection among criminals changed forever the way he understood the life we did not ask for and are reluctant to give up. Years after his release, he wrote a fiction based on his internment which he called the *House of the Dead*, and then a series of novels that gave expression to what he had learned. My mother's favorite author, Marcel Proust, said of these works that they could all be contained under a single title: *The Story of a Crime*. It was a crime committed by men who did not believe in God, but did not therefore believe in nothing. Instead, they believed in themselves as gods.

Dostoevsky understood the dilemma we face if our existence has no meaning. He asked himself whether a human life is possible in such a world, and answered that it was not. "Neither a man nor a nation can live without a 'higher idea,'" he wrote, adding: "There is only one such idea on this earth, that of an immortal human soul; all the other 'higher ideas' by which men live flow from that...."

In the great religious novel he wrote at the end of his life, Dostoevsky put this observation in the mouth of the character Ivan Karamazov, a tormented intellect who resembles the author, and struggles to believe against what he knows: "It is only men's belief in the immortality of their own souls that makes it possible for them to love one another, for morality to exist."

This is another way of saying that in order to be moral, men must inhabit stories that have no end. For if we are not immortal, and do not fear a judgment beyond ourselves what will we not do to satisfy our desires? Of what are we not capable? The life of the world we know is dependent on one we can only guess at, and this invisible world (or our belief in it) is necessary in order for the world we inhabit to continue. Without faith in a God who cares about us, "not only love, but also any living power to continue the life of the world would at once dry up: nothing would be immoral any longer; everything would be permitted."

The idea that we must be watched in order to behave is unflattering, and atheists find it repugnant. But does that make it false? Atheists may deny that we must fear judgment in order to act morally, but an agnostic can wonder all the same. What assurance is there that we will make virtuous choices in an existence that is brief, and unrequited, and full of temptation? Has there ever been in the history of humanity a community able to maintain order without the threat of punishment, whether here or in the hereafter?

It is true, as atheists will observe, that we often behave well when no one is watching. But *will* we? Will we do so when our backs are to the wall, and our survival is at stake? If the circumstances are right, who among us can be certain of his limits? On the fields of war where no law exists to keep men in check, it is well known that they will engage in unspeakable depravities. Each of us will want to regard ourselves as exceptions to the rule, and many will refrain from committing the worst of crimes. Perhaps there are even saints who walk among us. But what of it? It is still the rule.

Atheists will also object that religion is no cure for our sins since those who believe will act as badly as those who don't. But who would deny that a religious faith is no proof against sin? It is a truth the faithful themselves concede and make the focus of their concern. Moreover, the objection does not begin to address the question of whether human beings can be moral without the prospect of a judgment. In our daily lives we can hardly commit a selfish act without fearing discovery. Unless our moral compass is broken we will care what others think, and eyes will peep about in our heads to track what we do. We will even care about others' opinions of us after we are dead. How inexplicable is that?

In the end, the need to be watched is not merely about being good, but about being at all. My father did not believe in a God who numbers the hairs on every head. But he felt the need to be noted all the same. The god he worshipped was History and its eyes were always upon him. The audience of others, real or imagined, is the way we persuade ourselves that our drama has no end, and what we do matters. For if there is only the abyss in front of us and behind, what can matter other than the way in which we bring the curtain down?

XI

While Dostoevsky was a prisoner, a woman he did not know sent him a copy of the New Testament as a charity. He kept the book under his pillow until his sentence was complete. On his release he wrote the woman a note thanking her for the kindness, and offering this confession: "I tell you that there are moments in which one thirsts for faith like parched grass, ... and finds it for the very reason that truth shines more clearly in affliction."

Like Ivan Karamazov, who provided a fictional voice for his doubts, Dostoevsky never did find release. He was a child of his age, he explained to his benefactor, "a child of unbelief and doubt up to this very moment and (I am certain of it) to the grave. Nevertheless, God sends me moments of complete tranquility. In such moments I love and find that I am loved by others, and in such moments I have nurtured in myself a symbol of truth, in which everything is clear and holy for me. The symbol is very simple. It is the belief that there is nothing finer, profounder, more attractive, more reasonable, more courageous and more perfect than Christ."

A Jew might be expected to be cold to this affirmation, but I am not. It is a devotion we find in all religious faiths. Dostoevsky called the adoration of God a "touching of other worlds" more perfect than ours. From an agnostic's view, it doesn't really matter whether the perfection is imagined or real. If it is embraced, its effect is the same. A modern writer, Cormac McCarthy, has expressed the paradox this way: "In the end we shall all of us only be what we have made of God."

Can we dispense with this reverence for impossible worlds as atheists insist we must? Dostoevsky's answer is that we cannot. Without belief in the immortality of souls, "not only love, but also any living power to continue the life of the world would at once dry up." What can he have meant by this? Perhaps that if we were not inspired by an ideal world we would be reduced to the savagery of this one. Or, if we did not look forward to something better, we would not look forward at all.

Perhaps that is why he also wrote: "Even if someone were to prove to me that the truth lay outside Christ, I should prefer to remain with Christ than with the truth."

XII

Dostoevsky's belief in a divine truth set him apart from the other radicals awaiting their execution on that December morning. Standing in the line in front of him was a co-conspirator named Nikolay Speshnev, an atheist whom Dostoevsky later came to regard as the devil incarnate. As the two approached the scaffold area, Dostoevsky whispered to him, "We shall be with Christ." But the condemned man rejected his comfort, and pointing to the ground said: "A handful of dust."

Because he did not believe in God, however, Speshnev did not therefore believe in nothing. Like Dostoevsky, he too yearned to touch more perfect worlds, and like the other radicals awaiting their sentence he was willing to sacrifice his life for his ideals. The future they imagined was a world ordered by harmony and justice. Of their hope, Speshnev said: "[This] is also a religion only a different one. It makes a divinity out of a new and different object, but there is nothing new about the deification itself."

There was indeed nothing original about this conceit, which was shared by all the prophets of the new creed who regarded socialism as the answer to the religions that had failed. The "God" of traditional faith they viewed as a primitive fantasy born of human ignorance and weakness. Religious belief provided obvious comfort but a false one. Such belief prompted human beings to surrender their birthright and project onto a Divinity powers that were rightfully theirs—first onto many gods and then onto one. Under the spell of religious belief, they had alienated their human virtues, which were reason and compassion, and then worshipped them as attributes of a Divinity beyond reach. Thus religion deprived them of the power to change the circumstances of their lives and alter their fates. Religious faith was not a consolation for human unhappiness but its cause.

This radical idea is today the faith of millions of atheists but it makes no sense. Human beings do not project onto God the powers they have but rather the ones they do not have. The love that Dostoevsky associates with Christ is not an attribute of human beings or even something that is possible for them, as he explains: "To love man *as oneself* … is impossible; the ego stands in the way."

Dostoevsky inscribed these words on the funeral bier of his first wife, a morbid gesture but a revealing one. "Christ's love for people," he also said, "is in its kind a miracle impossible on earth; he was God, but we are not gods." These words reflect a conservative view of our human lot, the very opposite of the radical faith that we can become as gods, and create a new world.

A religious ideal can be useful if properly served. Rather than alienate human beings from their ability to love, the trust in a compassionate God may enhance, and even foster it.

What of the claim that religious faith breeds ignorance, and creates barriers to knowledge? It is certainly the case that ignorant people embrace ignorant forms of faith and the intolerant have often invoked religion to oppose the advance of science. But the architects of the scientific enlightenment—Copernicus, Pascal, and Newton—were all religious believers. It was precisely their faith in a supernatural design that inspired them to search for an order in the cosmos. Spinoza, Locke, and Kant, the avatars of the Age of Reason, also drew their inspiration from the lodestar of divinity and the belief in a providential design.

XIII

Speshnev did not think there was much difference between the faith of atheist radicals and faith in a supernatural being, between a secular hope that humanity could achieve its own redemption and a religious faith that only a divinity can save us. He asked rhetorically: "Is the difference between a God-man and a man-God really so great?"

Dostoevsky was sure it was. His alarm at the consequences of Speshnev's idea became the principal theme of his art. The centerpiece of his novel, *Crime and Punishment*, is the story of a murder. A student deliberately kills an old woman, whom he considers useless and even harmful, to prove to himself that he has the self-possession and will to change the world. The police inspector who tracks him down describes the murder as "a fantastic, gloomy business, a modern case," and identifies its cause as a mind directed by "bookish dreams" and "a heart unhinged by theories."

The murderer has written an academic essay, "On Crime," in which he explains the deed he is about to commit. Humanity, he writes, is divided into two groups. On the one hand, there are the masses who accept a morality that binds them to the existing order. On the other, there are the members of the radical vanguard "who seek in various ways the destruction of the present for the sake of the better." Among these innovators he mentions the imperial conquerors Napoleon and Mohammed, leaders of a secular faith and a religious one.

The quest for salvation breeds a self-righteousness that encourages radicals to commit crimes that are monstrous. "If such a one is forced for the sake of his idea to step over a corpse or wade through blood," Ivan Karamazov warns, "he can find in himself, *in his conscience*, a sanction for wading through blood." It is the nobility of the idea, the spectacular prospect of a world transformed that inspires and justifies the spectacular crimes.

Speshnev was hardly alone in identifying the utopian passion as a religious faith. Auguste Comte, who was one of the fathers of European socialism, called it a "religion of humanity." Of his fellow radicals, the anarchist Bakunin, said: "They are magnificent these young fanatics, believers without God...." Of these secular priests Dostoevsky wrote, they "talk of socialism or anarchism, or the transformation of all humanity on a new model so that it all comes to the same, the same questions turned inside out." But the same questions turned inside out lead to different answers. A God who becomes human and suffers in the flesh to redeem human sins is one thing; ordinary human beings acting as gods to purge others of their sins is quite another.

The radical vision of an earthly redemption requires ordinary mortals, fallible and corrupt, to assume powers that are god-like. Everything is permitted to them because everything can be justified as a service to humanity. "Socialism ... ," Dostoevsky wrote, "is a modern incarnation of godlessness, the tower of Babel built without God, not to raise earth to heaven but to bring heaven down to earth." Of social redeemers like this, he said, "they hope to make a just order for themselves, but having rejected Christ they will end by drenching the earth with blood."

XIV

The ancestors of my little Chihuahuas were called "Techichi" by the Aztecs, who revered them as gods and coveted them as indispensable guides to the land of the dead. The Aztecs were a people possessed by inordinate fear of their own extinction. The end of an ordinary day made them so anxious they came to believe that only the spilling of blood would cause the sun to rise again. To ensure their future, they held festivals of the sun in the temples of Tenochtitlan and cut out the hearts of thousands of virgins as an offering to the gods in the hope that it would protect them.

When an Aztec died, his survivors cremated him believing that souls were transported by fire and liberated by the flames. Along with the deceased they placed their dogs on the funeral pyres convinced that they would help the dead to navigate the nine rivers they believed lay between them and their final destination. Evidently, the Aztecs were also impressed by these dogs' ability to follow invisible trails.

Canines have been our companions since the Stone Age, surviving the millennia on the kindness of strangers. They were the first animals to be taken into human households, and the only ones to be so included in every society on earth. If you are attentive they will teach you humility, and will accompany you in your journey for a decade or more if you are lucky. Although there are no records to prove it, the Aztecs were obviously as enchanted as we are by the fidelity of these small souls, and their ardent affection for those who show them kindness. Unlike human beings, they will love you to the end, and will not abandon you before you reach it.

XV

The stories we tell ourselves to keep our souls in motion are numerous but their purpose is the same. Whether we imagine we are creating a family line that will continue forever, or are pursuing missions greater than ourselves whose effects will outlast us, whether we store up our illusions in personal albums or enshrine them in halls of fame, whether we record our days in intimate journals or official annals, every narrative is designed to convince us that what we do is noteworthy and that someone will be there to take it all in.

Every writer tells himself the same story—that someone is listening. A word on the page is one end of a silent conversation, but who is at the other? The English novelist Julian Barnes devoted an entire book to recording the anxieties provoked by the prospect that one day his words would no longer have readers and every trace of him would be gone. His book was an attempt to exorcise a lifelong obsession with his own extinction. He took its title from the advice his friends gave him as a child when he expressed fears about death: *Nothing To Be Frightened Of*. Barnes wrote the book when he was sixty, and said: "A novelist might hope for another generation of readers—two or three if lucky which may feel like a scorning of death; but it's really just a scratching on the wall of the condemned cell. We do it to say: I was here too."

But to whom?

CHAPTER TWO

NOVEMBER 2008

I

When my wife and I put the house in Calabasas up for sale, it was because we were looking for a property to stable horses. We had recently acquired a young gelding and rather than board him at a ranch a half hour distant, we wanted him close so that he would become part of our household. The new residence we were seeking would be the seventh I had occupied since April and I met twelve years earlier, and the fourth we had shared together. Although the move was a reflection of her passion rather than mine, this kind of transience was a recurrent theme of my life. Without exactly willing it, the many new residences I acquired and then abandoned had become an almost spiritual practice, preparing me for the day when it would be time to leave.

The new family member was an elegant paint with white flanks and chestnut markings, which were crowned by a fluted mane. Fine in the bone and with a demeanor that was almost feminine, Alvin was the missing piece of a life April wanted and I was determined to help her get. After months of searching we found a suitable location in the Santa Maria Valley, a green cut of the coastal range thirty miles to the north. Like Calabasas, its very name reflected the shifts of time, a landscape memorial to the ghosts of the Spanish past.

The spread we acquired was an acre-and-a-half set on two tiers of land, which was punctuated by a stand of pines. On the lower level there was a ranch-style house with a trellised veranda and wisteria vines covered in purple blooms; on the upper, a two-stall barn and pipe corrals for the horses backed by a large arena to exercise them in. The corrals were shaded by willowy pepper trees and faced by a row of rose bushes, the whole as congenial a setting as I could have hoped for, and I hoped it would be my last.

Because horses are herd animals, it was important that we acquire a companion for Alvin, which we quickly did. The new addition was a caramel draft pony whose name was Diddy, and whose blonde forelock and large brown eyes gave him a particularly endearing look. His breed was Haflinger of which it was said "a prince up front, a peasant behind," a reference to his formidable haunches. These were coupled with a chest so broad you could almost see the cart he was born to pull coming up behind him.

Millennia of attachment to human beings have not bred the wild out of horses. Consequently they demand discipline and patience until they acquire ground manners to make them safe, in which regard they are not unlike us. A combination of strength and vulnerability makes even the gentlest of these creatures a danger to those who do not understand their nature. Horses are flight animals who have been endlessly hunted through the corridors of time and are spooked by sights that are unfamiliar and by alien intrusions into their environment.

A car engine grinding or a squirrel darting into view can cause a half-ton of flesh to bolt in fear with a velocity that will crush anything in its path.

The muscular beauty of horses has inspired us to regard them as symbols of nobility, and the ancient Greeks even affixed the word "hippo" to their own names to appropriate an aristocratic aura. But the strength of equines is also deceptive since they are fragile in their construction. Their intestinal architectures make them prone to digestive disorders that can be fatal, while their massive weight is supported on ankles so narrow as to risk injuries that can bring them down as well.

Two months before we left the Calabasas house, Clifton—the horse across the way—developed a leg infection. It was unclear whether its cause was the steep incline of the hillside or an incompetent farrier who had improperly shoed him. As the days progressed, the infection spread until it brought his majestic frame to the ground. To behold so mighty a beast in such helpless agony was a wrenching sight, but it took days for his owner to recognize she was torturing a creature she loved, and finally to call in the vet to put him to rest.

II

Before arriving in our new home, we prepared the building by opening up cathedral ceilings in the master bedroom and living room, laying walnut floors, framing the windows and putting decorative finishes on the interior doors. We hired a crew to cut back the overgrowth on the grounds, paint the barn and tack room red, and put a white fence around the horse arena. It was the fourth home we had remodeled together. We had even gone so far as to renovate the house in Calabasas, which was a new construction when we settled in. Did this reflect a compulsive human need to make the world a better place? Or was it just our scratching on the wall?

Some of the alterations we made to the Calabasas property began with practical agendas, including the pool we built in the back yard. My routines as a writer were sedentary, and except for the walks with the dogs I engaged in no activity calculated to keep my engine running. This lassitude became a problem when I was diagnosed with diabetes and warned by my doctor that I would have to shed weight and exercise or risk troubling complications. Swimming had always been a pleasure for me, and building a pool seemed a happy way to fulfill his prescriptions, although we quickly embellished the plan with superfluous fountains, a garden and artificial rocks crafted to look like granite.

The diabetes that afflicted me was not the inherited kind, and while still a cause for concern, was less threatening. A medical website for laymen provided this information: "In Type II diabetes, either the body does not produce enough insulin or the cells ignore the insulin. When you eat food, the body breaks down all of the sugars and starches into glucose, which is the basic fuel for the cells in the body. Insulin takes the sugar from the blood into the cells. When glucose builds up in the blood instead of going into cells, it can cause two problems: 1) Right away, your cells may be starved for energy. 2) Over time, high blood glucose levels may hurt your eyes, kidneys, nerves, or heart." In good bedside fashion, the authors of the website finished these details with a reassuring uplift. "Finding out you have diabetes is scary. But don't panic. Type II diabetes is serious, but people with diabetes can live long, healthy, happy lives."

In other words, my eyes, kidneys, nerves, and heart were under attack, and my energy was in danger of being shut off, but not to worry. And for the most part I did not.

I adjusted to the inevitable and put myself on a diet. I selected the carbohydrates at the supermarket nutritionists said were "complex," lost enough weight to make the routine tests reassuring for my doctor, and used the pool daily. Overall, I considered myself lucky to have no symptoms and went on with my life as before. And what else was I to do?

Diabetes is a condition familiar to Jews, and my father had suffered from the disease in its more serious version, and required medication to keep it under control. Although the memory has faded, I can still see him standing in the family bathroom, his pants dropped around his ankles administering an insulin shot to his bared thigh. He conducted this procedure in the clinical manner with which he attended to all medical issues and household emergencies, creating a calm around them so that none of us paid particular notice to his condition.

III

Four years before our move to Calabasas I received a second more serious diagnosis when I was told I had a prostate cancer. I addressed the news more casually than I probably should have, perhaps under the influence of my father's example. Perhaps I felt the gods had been good to me until then and would see me through this trial as well. But my wife who was twenty years younger was not so sanguine. Her own horizon was still distant and expanding, and she feared my premature departure.

During the operation to remove the tumor, my surgeon detected what he thought was leakage through the prostate wall and ordered radiation to destroy cells that may have escaped. It was "just a precaution" but later tests indicated that traces of the disease had lingered. There was no therapy for this, but it was also not clear whether these cells would cause me any more trouble than the many effects of age that eventually bring us down. While my wife fretted, the doctors maintained their professional serenity and reassured us that the prostate cancer would probably be outrun by other forces that nature had put in place to do the job.

My maternal grandfather died from a stomach cancer in his seventies, and my father who was a heavy smoker had developed a cancer of the tongue in his mid-forties; but after undergoing radium treatments he was able to continue for another forty years. My prostate cancer was unrelated to either case, and consequently I again confronted a medical puzzle when inquiring into its source.

It was not until eight years after the operation that I received a possible answer when my friend Peter sent me an email containing a newspaper report about a virus researchers believed was the cause of chronic fatigue syndrome, a malady I had contracted in my mid-forties: "The new suspect is a xenotropic murine leukemia virus-related virus, or XMRV, which probably descended from a group of viruses that cause cancer in mice. How or when XMRV found its way into humans is unknown. But it has also been linked to cancer in people: it was first identified three years ago, in prostate cancer, and later detected in about one-quarter of biopsies from men with that disease...."

The illnesses that afflicted me were among many available, and I did not consider myself unfairly singled out. From the cursory research I conducted into my condition, I learned that everyone will develop a cancer if they live long enough. It was one more reminder that we were not built to last, and that age itself is a disease that overtakes us all.

IV

The Santa Maria Valley where we now lived was cradled between two columns of mountains, which rose from its floor like green waves frozen in space and time. An agricultural plain lay between them with orange and lemon groves on one side of the flat and a warren of horse communities on the other. Ours was gated, and I took my exercise walks with the dogs along the squared streets at the end of our driveway. The walks were infrequent now because the new property was big enough to provide sufficient space for the dogs to roam without me. Several times a day I let them run loose on the tree-shaded lawn at the back of the house where they chased horses and dogs passing on the other side of the fence. During their romps I would sit on the veranda and keep a watchful eye out for coyotes and hawks on the hunt for small animals in the neighborhood yards.

I no longer had a pool for a daily swim but made up for the missed exertions with new chores, pitching hay to the horses and lunging them in trots around the arena. April took charge of the paint, and I assumed responsibilities for the draft pony with whom I had developed an affectionate bond. Lunging Diddy was important because he was carrying extra pounds that put him at risk for colic or foundering. He enjoyed the runs and missed them when I was too busy with other tasks. My days now were largely spent with the animals and in the solitary writing projects that were my principal work. I settled happily into these pleasures, embraced their slower pace and tried not to be concerned about the future.

V

The stories that comfort us are parables of hope. Some are personal and are designed to generate memories that outlive us. Others extend beyond ourselves and promise a transformation of the world we know into one that makes sense. These are the myths of faith, both secular and religious, that shape our histories, and it is no trivial matter whether the future they promise is of this world or the next.

The choice of futures is rooted in our view of origins. Belief in a redemption in the next life can only spring from the conviction that our very nature is corrupt in this one. For if the cause of our suffering lies within us, the only hope we can have of salvation is a divine intervention. By contrast, those who strive for a redemption in *this* life must believe that the cause of our unhappiness does not lie in our nature but in the world outside us, which we are destined to correct.

Dostoevsky was a man of faith and believed that the source of human misery lay in our corruption. But he also saw that the root of this corruption was the freedom that made us human. This is the theme of his most famous fiction, "The Grand Inquisitor," a fable told by Ivan Karamazov.

Ivan's tale is set in the sixteenth century and begins with a prelude, in which he observes that more than a millennium has passed since Christ promised to return in His glory. In the story that follows, Christ returns to His creation but with no intention of resolving the uncertainty provoked by His absence, which has left His creatures without answers to the questions that trouble them most. The Inquisitor has Christ arrested, and denounces Him as the "worst of heretics" whose very presence threatens the authority of the Church, His ministry on earth.

Ivan's fable is the trial of God for the crime of creation. In giving human beings freedom, God is the true source of our unhappiness. For "nothing has ever been more insupportable for a man and a human society than freedom." By refusing to enter history and compel belief, God has condemned His children to live alone and lost, not knowing why they are here, or where they are going, or whether what they do or who they are has any significance at all.

Out of compassion for God's abandoned creatures, the Inquisitor informs Christ that the Church of Rome has undertaken the mission of an earthly redemption that He rejected. It has set out to repair the fault in creation and to provide human beings with the earthly happiness and security that has been denied them. But in exercising dominion over worldly things, the Church has also entered the realm of corruption, which is the devil's domain.

"We are working not with Thee, but with *him* …," the Inquisitor tells Christ, as he reflects on the temptations the devil offered Him in the desert, which He rejected: "We took from him what thou didst reject with scorn, that last gift he offered Thee, when he showed Thee all the kingdoms of the earth. We took from Rome and the sword of Caesar, and proclaimed ourselves sole rulers of the earth…. We shall triumph and shall be

Caesars, and then we shall plan the universal happiness of man."

Satan's offer was made to Christ in the form of three temptations: to turn the stones into bread; to cast Himself from a height and thus prove He was immortal; to rule over the kingdoms of the earth. To accept any of the three would prove that He *was* God, and compel belief. Ivan describes the three temptations as expressing "the whole future of the world and of humanity." The three are really one: to give up freedom for security and happiness.

"You had the power to turn the stones into bread," the Inquisitor scolds Christ, "for which they would have given you their souls. But you refused. What sort of freedom is it, you reasoned, if obedience is bought with loaves of bread?"

Christ had rejected Satan's temptation saying, "Man does not live by bread alone, but by every word that proceeds out of the mouth of the Lord." The Inquisitor agrees. "The secret of man's being is not only to live but to have something to live for. Without a stable conception of the object of life, man would not consent to go on living, and would rather destroy himself than remain on earth, though he had bread in abundance." The Church provides its followers with a meaning for their existence through the authority and mystery of its doctrines. All that is required to enter its earthly paradise is submission to its faith.

If there are no words from heaven to provide meaning for men's lives but only silence, if they are fated to live in uncertainty, what then? Will they believe in nothing? Or is the need to have something to live for so powerful they will believe in a gospel that promises them both happiness *and* bread?

This is the Inquisitor's answer: not only will they worship the power that promises them bread and earthly happiness, but they will prefer it to a divinity who would set them free: "You objected that man does not live by bread alone, but do you know that in the name of this very earthly bread, the spirit of the earth will rise against you and fight with you and defeat you, and everyone will follow him exclaiming, 'Who can compare to this beast, for he has given us the fire from heaven?' They will lay their freedom at our feet and say to us, 'Make us your slaves, but feed us.'"

Dostoevsky's Inquisitor is the spokesman for all the tyrannies that have existed from the beginning of time, and that have oppressed mankind in the name of progress. Speaking in a public lecture about his novel, Dostoevsky described his Inquisitor as an atheist who "distort[s] the truth of Christ by identifying it with the aims of this world." In making the kingdom of heaven the work of human beings, he explained, "the sublime Christian view of mankind is reduced to regarding humanity as if it were an animal herd, and under the guise of a social love of mankind there appears a scarcely masked contempt for it."

The earthly paradise that ordinary mortals create is not the kingdom of freedom but the totalitarian state. For how could the human beings we know become new men and new women without gods to oversee them? How could they live in harmony? "Freedom and bread enough for all are inconceivable together," the Inquisitor admonishes Christ, "for never, never will they be able to share between them!" Without the subservience of those who are to be redeemed, how can the redeemers hope to create a new heaven and a new earth? The church of socialism cannot allow its flock the freedom to oppose its redemption. But this is the one freedom that leads to all others.

Human beings are destined to be unhappy, the Inquisitor explains to Christ, until they "know the value of complete submission." Once they embrace this, "once they are made to submit, we shall give them the quiet humble happiness of weak creatures such as they are by nature.... We shall have an answer for all. And they will be glad to believe our answer, for it will save them from the great anxiety and terrible agony they endure in making a free decision for themselves."

VI

When we moved to the Santa Maria Valley, I was already approaching my sixty-ninth year. In a synchronicity of fate, my dogs had reached a similar point along their downward arcs. But while I was only mildly curious about the oldster who looked at me from the bathroom mirror each morning, I was saddened to see the signs of age on them, to note the wrinkled jowls and graying hairs, grim reminders of the destination they would reach before me.

The familiarities of the passing years had bred in us greater understanding of each other. Lucy had always displayed a feral deference to me as the alpha of her pack, averting her eyes when in proximity to mine and positioning herself at respectful but frustrating distances when the two of us were alone. However, as the years progressed this diffidence began to fade, and she would often slip up alongside me to allow herself a gaze that was touchingly direct. Out of the corner of my eye I would catch hers, then return her look and be surprised to see her lock into mine and remain. I warmed to this closeness but it also increased the sadness I felt anticipating the end, which only I knew was coming.

Snug inside our stories, we take our worlds for granted and assume they will continue indefinitely. We create our families and plot our bloodlines as though they will go on and on, and when we bury our dead, we promise to remember them forever, although it is a promise we know we cannot keep.

When the musical genius Mozart was thirty-one he had created hundreds of works of indescribable beauty, imparting happiness to countless individuals who came after him including myself. But he was already only four years from the end of his life. While working on his famous *Requiem Mass*, he was stricken with a fatal illness that would easily be cured today. His death, which came swiftly, has been rightly called the greatest tragedy in the history of music, depriving us and generations not born of pleasures we can hardly imagine.

In his thirty-first year, Mozart wrote a letter to his father who was then drawing his own last breaths. In it he said: "As death (considered precisely) is the real purpose of our life, for several years I have become closely acquainted with this true and best friend of our life, so that his image is not only no longer terrifying to me, but rather something very soothing and comforting!" Then he added: "And I thank my God for affording me, in His grace, the opportunity (you understand me) of realizing that He is the key to our real happiness. I never lie down in bed without thinking that (young as I am) I may not live to see the next day—and yet no one, especially among those who know me, can say that in daily life I am stubborn or sad—and for this happiness I give thanks to my Creator every day and wish every man the same from the bottom of my heart...."

It is a generous thought from a miraculous soul. I wish the faith of this great and gifted young man were mine as well. I wish I could place my trust in the hands of a Creator. I wish I could look on my life and the lives

of my children and all I have loved and see them as pre-
ludes to a better world. But, try as I might, I cannot. And
so I am left to ponder the pointlessness of our strivings
on this earth and to ask impossible questions, and receive
no answers.

VII

Of my four children and their futures, I worried most
about my oldest daughter, Sarah, who was born with a
genetic condition that saddled her with great burdens.
These included problems that affected her hearing, her
sight, and her heart. An early death was predicted for
those born with her condition, but her life was so full that
we who loved her forgot the sentence. Then, two months
after her forty-fourth birthday, I received a call from her
sister Anne who said, "Something terrible has happened."
And then, "Sarah is gone."

There is nothing more irrevocable than the grave, and
no loss ever left me so desolate. With that phone call my
life entered a sudden winter from which there would be
no release. All that was left to me were the images of
times we shared together, which were gone and which I
could not get back. Like other mourners, I was overcome

by the feeling that if she had indeed gone to a better place, as many who tried to comfort me were persuaded, I would be relieved to join her.

My daughter's death inverted nature's order and was a violent rebuke to every parental instinct. Among the afflictions of mourning were the memories of our conversations that had been left unfinished, which I longed to continue. Yet what was this longing, itself so futile, since all our conversations are unfinished?

My daughter was a writer and an observant Jew, and just before her death she was interviewed by a literary magazine. The interviewer asked whether her religious practice helped her to deal with the recent death of an aunt with whom she was particularly close. "I think it did," she answered, adding that she was "very comfortable," with the idea that Judaism didn't have a highly developed concept of an after-life. Religion was an effort to find meaning "and I think at the heart of that pursuit is the fact that we all walk around with the knowledge that we are going to die."

Her words on the page gave me a start. In her father's eyes she was too young to have thought so deeply about such dark matters. But on reflection I realized what should have been obvious—that these thoughts were her birthright. It was her mother and I who had suppressed the warning of an early death. One of the bits of information she provided the interviewer was that every day over her breakfast coffee she recited the Jewish prayer of mourning: *You resurrect the dead*. She did not believe in a literal resurrection, she explained, but in what she called a "rolling of the souls," a reincarnation of the departed spirit in others.

My daughter never married but lived alone in a one-bedroom apartment and left behind piles of manuscripts which she had worked on as a writer, and which with the exception of a single poem had never been published. Her papers included many volumes of a notebook and diary she kept, along with shopping bags full of stories and poems in various states of revision. There were also many versions of a novel, which she had worked on for twenty years and which she called *The Carousel of Time*, and then *The Family of Man*. All these scraps represented the uncollected pieces of my daughter's life, the hours she spent by herself day and night to complete works that were now a scattered debris on her apartment floor.

Many would feel sadness at the apparent futility of my daughter's efforts, but I do not. For how different is this than the futility all of us share whether our works are published or not, and whether our efforts are expended alone or in the company of others? How different were the tasks my daughter undertook from those of the most famous authors whose works are read by millions and who will one day leave their own debris behind?

When I ask myself why I rise in the morning to write this page and spend the time that time will soon erase, my answer is this: on the days when the words fall into place and an order appears, I am at peace. Thus, it was actually a relief when I saw how my daughter had spent her hours arranging words on a page and transforming her world into one that made sense. I knew then she was happy and at peace.

My daughter was also right about the rolling of the souls. Wherever I go, thoughts of her follow me, and my future takes on a memory and a face.

VIII

It is humbling to look into historical texts and see how images of the past that have been recorded by others are familiar to us, and how little we have learned from their experience. Dostoevsky's *Diary of a Writer,* which was published more than a hundred years ago, contains this reminiscence: "'Do you know,' Belinsky screeched one evening (sometimes, if he was very excited, he would screech) as he turned to me, 'Do you know that man's sins cannot be counted against him? ... When society is set up in such a mean fashion ... man cannot help but do wrong; economic factors alone lead him to do wrong; and it is absurd and cruel to demand from a man something the very laws of nature make it impossible for him to carry out, even if he wanted to.'"

Belinsky's outburst took place in the course of an evening at the circle of St. Petersburg radicals that Dostoevsky had joined. Thirty years later, Dostoevsky wrote about the incident. He regarded Belinsky's remark that evening as so important that he also incorporated it into the creed of the church of socialism. Ivan's Grand Inquisitor confronts Christ with this prophecy: "Do you know that centuries will pass and mankind will proclaim with the mouth of its wisdom and science that there is no crime, and therefore no sin, but only hungry men? 'Feed them first, then ask virtue of them!'—that is what they will write on the banner they raise against you, and by which your temple will be destroyed."

By the time Dostoevsky had reached the end of his days he was so revered by his countrymen that he had become a national symbol, and was regarded by them as a prophet. Yet no one really listened. In less than an individual's lifetime, socialist radicals seized power in St. Petersburg, and renamed it "Leningrad," raising to sainthood the malevolent dictator who decided the fate of millions. Under the rule of Leninists, Russia became the center of a revolution to create a new world and to fashion new human beings to inhabit it. These miracles were to be achieved by transforming Belinsky's "economic factors."

During Russia's bloody upheavals, the Communist playwright Bertolt Brecht took the very words the Inquisitor had spoken—"First comes feeding, then comes morality"—and inserted them into a popular German opera intending to inspire others to join the revolutionary cause. When the destructive energies of the revolution had run their course they left in their wake a hundred million corpses and blighted the lives of many more. But the fantasy of a socialist paradise lived on.

There is no secret to Dostoevsky's clairvoyance. He understood that morality was not the product of feeding human beings but was an expression of their humanity and their freedom. The radical view expressed by Belinsky is that we are the products of social engineering and thus constructed by our environment. This is the heart of all schemes for an earthly redemption, and the antithesis of freedom. It is the philosophy, as Dostoevsky put it, of an anthill. In his *Diary*, he answered Belinsky: "In making the individual dependent on every flaw in the social structure, ... the doctrine of the environment reduces the subject to an absolute non-entity, exempting him totally from every personal moral duty and from all independence, reduces him to the lowest form of slavery imaginable."

IX

When criminals are viewed as society's victims, the crimes they commit can be seen as a form of social justice. "Since society is organized in such a vile fashion," Belinsky explained on that memorable evening, "one can only break out of it with a knife in hand." To the social redeemers, criminals are "unfortunates," since the responsibility for their crimes lies in society itself. Dostoevsky described their thinking this way: "Society is vile, and therefore we too are vile; but we are rich, we are secure, and it is only by chance we escaped encountering the things you did. And had we encountered them, we would have acted as you did. Who is to blame? The environment is to blame. And so, there is only a faulty social structure, but there is no crime whatsoever."

From such attitudes it is a small step to regarding those who break the law as social heroes, or to describe them with the term fashionable in Dostoevsky's time as "people's criminals." They break the law to achieve "people's justice." Thus revolutionaries seeking to change the world do not see the targets of their violence as human beings like themselves but as "enemies of the people" who have earned their fate.

When Dostoevsky came to write a novel about political radicals, he called it *The Devils* and modeled its central figure on a Russian terrorist named Sergei Nechaev. A colleague of Bakunin's, Nechaev founded an organization called "People's Justice," for which he wrote a "Catechism for Revolutionaries." In the course of his political activities Nechaev induced his small circle of followers to kill a student in their group in order to seal their revolutionary bond in blood. In the "Catechism for Revolutionaries," he elevated expediency to a moral principle. The goal revolutionaries were seeking of a world transformed justified any means necessary to achieve it: "Poison, the knife, the noose.... The revolution sanctifies everything...."

The creed of the revolutionary divides the world into forces of good and evil—on the one side enemies of the people, on the other the social redeemers. The passion to create a new world is really a passion to destroy the old one, transforming the love of humanity into a hatred for the human beings who stand in its way.

X

Nine months after we buried my daughter in a gravesite south of San Francisco, I arranged to have dinner with her rabbi, Alan Lew. We met at the Millennium Restaurant, which was one of Sarah's favorites. Rabbi Lew was a kind and thoughtful man who had written a book about the Jewish days of repentance and awe. In the Jewish calendar these are the days set aside to reflect upon one's life. The rabbi called his book, *This Is Real and You Are Completely Unprepared.*

Lew was five years younger than I and had no warning at the time of our dinner that he had only two more weeks to live. Like Sarah, he left behind an unpublished manuscript on which he had been laboring for over thirty years. It was a detailed history of his family beginning with his great-great-grandparents, who had been born in Russia and were the earliest of the Lews that any family member still alive could remember. The Lew children fled the war in Europe to find a better life across the sea, and to bear their children on American soil.

It had taken Rabbi Lew all those thirty years to track down his family survivors and record their stories. At dinner he told me that he had just put the finishing touches on his manuscript and sent it to a publisher. He called his book, *The Life That Ran Through Me.*

On my way to meet the rabbi, I had to walk up one of San Francisco's famous hills to the Millennium. This modest effort spiked a pain in the middle of my chest similar to the stitch one feels in the winter cold when the oxygen is thin. The pain recurred the next evening while

I was ascending a ramp at a sporting event and again the following day when I returned to Los Angeles and had to drag my luggage across a parking lot in the Burbank airport. A heartache is not necessarily life threatening, but the recurrence three times in as many days was a warning I sensed would be unwise to ignore. While still in the airport parking lot, I pulled my cell phone from the jacket I was wearing and called my doctor who told me to head straight for the emergency room at the local hospital and check myself in.

An angina is a strangling of the heart and can sneak up on you when you least expect it. The cause is often a clogged artery, and an episode can be brought on by ordinary events such as a physical exertion or emotional distress, or even a heavy meal, all of which require extra effort from the pump and more fuel than the blocked vessels can supply. After taking my vital signs and listening to my story, the cardiologist assigned to my case ordered an angiogram to see what was there. When his camera located the block, he inserted a stent to open the passage and restore the flow. The blockage was in the left anterior descending artery, which doctors mordantly refer to as "the widow-maker," but there was no damage to the heart, and I was released from the hospital after a day.

I was back home a little over a week when I learned of Rabbi Lew's collapse. He had taken a trip to Baltimore and was jogging to keep his heart healthy when it gave out. The body was flown back to San Francisco, and they buried him in the same cemetery as my daughter, a few feet to the right of her grave. We are here, and we are gone, and everything with us. No more jogs for the heart or books to complete, or dinners with family and friends. The stories simply stop, and all the loose ends are left untied.

XI

I began my rehabilitation on a treadmill I bought as a preventive measure to forestall future attacks. The cardiologist put me on a regimen of blood thinners and beta-blockers and let me know again how fortunate I was to have survived the episode without any damage to the organ itself. Even though I am not one to run to the outer edge of an anxiety and conclude the worst, the attack was not something I could just put behind me. It was a reminder that life is fragile, and I was not going to be here forever, which is something that is surprisingly easy to forget.

Once again, I was curious about the origins of the disease that had struck me, since there was no history of heart problems in my family. But the doctors had no answers. Scientific research had established that a case of diabetes increased the possibility of heart attacks, but no one knew exactly how. It made me wonder on particularly unsettling days whether my inattention to dietary matters or weakness for desserts was adversely affecting the span I had left.

A heart disease is not like a cancer, which moves silently and often slowly in one's bodily depths. The heart is a muscle near the surface making its signals of distress impossible to ignore. Nor can you put out of mind its ability to shut off everything quite suddenly like the flip of a switch.

When you are entering such uncharted terrain, the tremors of ordinary stress can be difficult to distinguish from a cardiac alarm. This left me for a while in a no man's land where I felt each day might produce a final call. Eventually I saw I was not as fragile as the angina had prompted me to feel and the dilemmas abated. While it lasted, however, the new level of uncertainty led to the thought that I should put my things in order so as not to burden my survivors more than necessary. But I quickly realized there was no chance of achieving even so modest a goal. Whatever I did and whenever I went there would be a mess left behind.

XII

While Dostoevsky was planning *The Devils*, he described his ideas for the novel in a letter to a friend. He intended to encapsulate its theme, he said, in an epigraph taken from the gospel of Luke. The passage he chose concerned a man possessed by devils who had come to Jesus seeking release. "Now a large herd of swine was feeding there on the hillside; and the devils begged Jesus to let them enter them. Then the devils came out of the man and entered the swine, and the herd rushed down the steep bank into the lake and were drowned."

Dostoevsky explained the connection between this parable and the story he was writing to his friend: "The facts have shown us that the sickness that seized civilized Russians was much stronger than we ourselves imagined, and that the matter did not end with Belinsky ... But what occurred here is what was witnessed by the evangelist

Luke. Exactly the same thing happened with us: the devils came out of the Russian man and entered into a herd of swine, that is, into the Nechaevs...."

In the novel he eventually wrote, Dostoevsky described how the utopian idea plants itself in the minds of dreamers who are seeking to release the world from its suffering. But it quickly enters the bodies of radical swine who are bent on destruction, and who pursue it until eventually they destroy themselves.

Critics of the novel complained that Dostoevsky had maligned Russia's youth by associating them with violence and nihilism, saying that only the uneducated and society's marginal dregs could become Nechaevists, and commit such heinous crimes. Dostoevsky answered: "And why do you suppose that the Nechaevs must absolutely be fanatics? Very often they are simply scoundrels.... These scoundrels are very crafty and have thoroughly studied the magnanimous aspect of the human soul—and most often the soul of youth—so as to be able play on it as on a musical instrument...."

Dostoevsky knew the idealism of radicals and understood its malignant consequences because he had been a radical himself. "I myself am an old Nechaevist; I also stood on the scaffold condemned to death, and I assure you that I stood in the company of educated people." Almost all the members of his radical circle had graduated from institutions of higher learning, and some of them later made distinguished, even noteworthy contributions to fields of knowledge. "No, gentlemen," he warned, "the Nechaevists do not always come only from idlers who have never studied anything.... There was not a single 'monster' or 'scoundrel' among [us] ... whether we speak of those who stood on the scaffold or those who remain untouched...."

Then Dostoevsky turned to the paradox at the heart of the radical calling, the fact that it is the noble idea itself that inspires the passion to destroy. "In my novel *The Devils*, I attempted to depict those diverse and multifarious motives by which even the purest of hearts and the most innocent of people can be drawn into committing such a monstrous offense. And therein lies the real horror: that in Russia one can commit the foulest and most villainous act without being in the least a villain! And this happens not only in Russia but all over the world, and it has happened since time began...."

And was to happen again. Despite Dostoevsky's efforts to warn others, despite the fact that he was a national figure regarded as a prophet, the nihilistic idea that had captured his youth and nearly destroyed him became an inspiration for the next generation to lay waste his country and make it a desert:

> *Even in 1846 Belinsky had initiated me into the whole truth of this coming "reborn world" and into the whole sanctity of the future communist society. All these convictions of the immorality of the very foundations (Christian ones) of contemporary society and of the immorality of religion and the family; of the immorality of the right to private property; of the elimination of nationalities in the name of the universal brotherhood of people and of contempt for one's fatherland as something that only showed universal development, and so on and so forth—all these things were influences we were unable to resist and which, in fact, captured our hearts and minds in the name of something very noble.*

Nihilism in the name of something noble. And so it continues to this day, more than a hundred and fifty years later.

XIII

The Communists began their revolution in Russia by killing the Czar and his entire family down to the last guiltless child. The crime was necessary, they said, to liberate Russia from hereditary monarchy and the tyrannies of the past. To free Russia from religious superstition, they sacked the nation's 75,000 churches. To institute social justice they created a police state. To instill faith in reason they formed a "People's Church" and built it alongside the prison camps and execution blocks. The masses now worshipped not God but the Marxist leader who had liberated them from slavery, calling Stalin the "Genius of Humanity," and "The Father of the Peoples." In no time he became a thousandfold more powerful and ruthless than the Czars.

Nothing in Russia's new world was un-foretold, not even this. "So long as man remains free," the Inquisitor had warned, "he strives for nothing so incessantly and so painfully as to find someone to worship." For freedom is a torment, and a man who is free experiences "no greater anxiety than to find someone quickly to whom he can hand over that gift of freedom."

When the Soviet nightmare came to an end, the "Great Architect of Communism" who was drenched in rivers of his people's blood and had brought an entire nation to its knees, was still revered above all others. Stalin had killed and enslaved tens of millions, and reduced his entire country to unimaginable poverty. But without him, his victims felt naked and afraid. Though he had ordered the murder of virtually one member of every Russian family, millions attended his funeral cortege, and nearly a thousand of them were trampled to death by the frenzied throng that followed him to his final rest. To honor his memory, his victims mummified his body and put it on display. His Kremlin tomb became a national shrine. Legions of his benighted subjects made annual pilgrimages to pay homage to his glory. In a poll conducted fifty years after his death, Stalin was voted the third most popular Russian in his nation's history after Alexander Nevsky and Peter the Great.

As the Inquisitor observed, the human yearning for a higher authority is a collectivist passion, the desire to find "a community of worship." Dostoevsky called this "the chief misery of every man individually and of all humanity from the beginning of time." Driven by the desire to have everyone submit to one God, men have gone to war from time immemorial. Even as they seek desperately for a common object to love, so they yearn for a common enemy to hate, which is why the quest for an earthly redemption has led to the greatest crimes.

CHAPTER THREE

DECEMBER 2010

I

I have never been a collector of objects from the past, but through all the moves I have made and the losses I have suffered, I have managed to keep in my possession a faded photograph that was taken when I was still a toddler, barely three years old. In the photo I am standing in my shorts and suspenders with my head straining upwards at the figure of an immense equine. The picture was taken by my father during a family vacation in the country, and my mother catalogued it for the family album, inscribing the words "David and the Giant" on its obverse side. Among the thoughts this image provokes is this oddity: I have come to the end of an urban life to find myself nested in a rural setting in the company of horses; yet I feel as much at home here as in any place I have lived.

Ever since the time of the emperor Marcus Aurelius, a dwelling on the land among horses would be an odd circumstance for a Jew. When the Romans conquered Jerusalem they scattered its inhabitants to the four corners of the globe. Afterwards, Jews lived among strangers and were rarely ranchers or farmers. If the right to own land was not denied them, they also avoided it for practical reasons. Forced to settle among peoples who regarded them as infidels, they were perpetually on the alert for a hostile turn in the environment that would force them to move on. Over centuries of persecutions, they acquired the instincts of flight animals. Knowing that things could go very badly and quickly, they kept their assets liquid and their passports at hand.

At the turn of the last century, my grandparents became part of yet another Jewish exodus, fleeing from Moravia and the Ukraine to seek refuge in America, a country that offered itself as an exception to the historical rule. The American founders had separated church and state, and a Constitution devised by immigrants removed their status as intruders. Consequently, when I acquired a homestead in the Santa Maria Valley nearly two and a half centuries later, my little odyssey had no greater significance than the breaking of a family mold.

II

A Jewish wisdom suggests that when a human being dies a whole world is lost. Having observed my dogs over many years, I am sure this is true of animals as well. Within a single breed and even the same brood no two dogs can be said to be the same. My black and white spot, Jake, is perpetually on edge and shadows me like a bodyguard, afraid I might disappear. When I leave the house, he sits at the front window, a lone sentry awaiting my return. When he thinks I am about to leave he grows agitated and is unable to eat. If I put a dish in front of him, he jumps back as though it might strike him. At night I can hear the ticking of his nails across the hardwood floors and then the crunch of the food I have put out for him, as he eats in the safety of the dark.

Lucy is his polar opposite. She lunges to seize the food from my hand, and makes her own way about the house, perching on her favorite chair in regal isolation. When I let the dogs out in the yard, Jake is the last to venture forth and then only briefly for relief. Lucy bolts through the sliders and walks the far edges of the yard, stalking animals and neighbors as they pass, until I summon her back. I have no idea why their personalities are so different, but they are, and I know I will not be able to replace them when they are gone.

Chihuahuas attend to movements around them, and strange intrusions will cause their entire bodies to shake with fear. Bewildered by our absences and elated at our returns, their anxiety over the unknown future is not unlike the Aztecs' who took them as companions long ago. Not understanding what kind of beings we are, and unable to discern our purposes, how can these little dogs look on us as anything but gods?

The helplessness of these little creatures is a way to measure the gratuitous cruelties of which human beings are capable, and have been since the beginning of time. Not long ago the wife of a soldier away at war went on a shopping run. While she was out four young men broke into her house and ransacked it, stealing what they could, and turning her home into a rubble. As if the damage was insufficient, they lingered to play some additional pranks, urinating on the clothes in her closet. They then took her pet Chihuahua, shaking with uncomprehending fear, and shoved him into her freezer, and slammed the door shut.

III

"People speak sometimes about the 'animal cruelty' of man," Ivan Karamazov observed to his brother Alyosha who was studying to be a priest. "But that is terribly unjust and offensive to animals. No animal could ever be so cruel, so artfully, so artistically cruel."

The conversation between them is the substance of another chapter of *The Brothers Karamazov*, which Dostoevsky called "Rebellion," placing it before Ivan's fable of the Inquisitor. Its subject is Ivan's argument with God, his rebellion against the idea of a redemption that requires children to suffer. "Men have a great love of torturing children, even love children in that sense," he comments with a caustic irony. "It is the defenselessness of these creatures that tempts the torturers, the angelic trustfulness of the child who has nowhere to run and no one to turn to...."

The suffering of the innocent and the torments of the helpless provide Ivan with a case against the future harmony of mankind that Christians are promised. His meticulously collected examples begin with a newspaper account of Muslim soldiers in the Balkans cutting the unborn from their mothers' wombs and tossing nursing infants onto the points of their bayonets. He then cites a newspaper report describing an eight-year-old boy who has been tortured to death by the master of his estate. The boy, whose parents are serfs, had inadvertently injured a favorite dog. Irate, the master orders the shivering child to be stripped naked in the arctic winter, then commands his hunting dogs to attack the terrified victim and tear him to pieces.

Ivan asks Alyosha to consider the reconciliation of all with all that God has promised. While the mother of the child may forgive the torturer for her own suffering, she has no right, Ivan argues, to forgive him for the suffering of her child. And if that is the case what universal harmony, and therefore what redemption, is possible?

Ivan is referring to a redemption in the hereafter. But what does the wanton cruelty of human beings, their love for the suffering of others, say about the possibility of a redemption in *this* life? Human perversity is such that not merely strangers but parents will abuse and torture their children. Ivan is ready with examples. For inadvertently soiling her bed, a girl of five is beaten without mercy by her mother and father, who are educated people: "They beat her, flogged her, kicked her, not knowing why themselves, until her whole body was nothing but bruises. Finally they attained the height of finesse: in the freezing cold, they locked her all night in the outhouse, because she wouldn't ask to get up and go in the middle of the night (as if a five-year-old child sleeping its sound angelic sleep could have learned to ask by that age). For that they smeared her face with her excrement and made her eat her excrement, and it was her mother, her mother who made her! And this mother could sleep while her poor little child was moaning all night in that vile place."

In the foul and freezing dark the little girl had prayed. "Can you understand," Ivan cries, "that a small creature, who cannot even comprehend what is being done to her, in a vile place, in the dark and the cold, beats herself on her strained little chest with her anguished, gentle, meek tears for 'dear God' to protect her—can you understand such nonsense, my friend and my brother, my godly and humble novice, can you understand why this nonsense is needed and created?"

It is the same question that Job puts to the God of the Old Testament, and that men of religious faith have asked since the beginning of time: if there is evil, how can the creator of the world not be its author? And yet how can He permit it? How can a God of perfect love be the author of perfect hate? Ivan finds the thought unbearable. If human harmony requires the suffering of one innocent child, he berates his brother, it is "too high a price, ... and so I return my entrance ticket."

Despite Ivan's rebellion, believers can still maintain their faith by appealing to the limited horizons of our mortal estate. We see through the glass darkly, ignorant of God's plan. Since His design is incomprehensible to us, the possibility persists that it may yet prove just. Through this logic, believers can hold onto their faith, which they do because otherwise they could not go on.

Atheists will scorn this choice as the consolation of the weak. But is their scorn well placed? If believers confront a dilemma that seems insoluble, consider the problem encountered by those who lack their belief. To create a world that is harmonious and just, secular redeemers must put their trust in human beings. But how can human beings create themselves anew? A glance at the human record reveals this to be a much greater leap of faith than relying on a hidden God. Divinity is by nature unknowable, but we are known and our ways familiar. Unless we are in denial, we cannot doubt what the outcome will be.

Consider that those who worship a God of perfection will want to obey His moral law. In seeking to bring about a general happiness they will resist the sacrifice of the innocent. But what moral authority restrains the redeemers who speak in the name of a virtuous future? To what God do they answer when they are tempted to shed blood for a greater good?

Would human beings have imagined a world of bliss if the one they had created were not so heartless? What is the ground, then, for the hope that they can create a world that is different? How can creatures so consumed with hate, and so steeped in blood, fashion their own salvation?

IV

In the Oval Office of the American White House, a wheat-colored rug has been installed with this testament to the progressive faith: "The arc of the universe is long but it bends towards justice."

But does it? How do innocents fare today as compared to the reactionary past? Terrible as the examples Dostoevsky provides, they do not begin to touch the limits of human depravity. In this modern and presumably enlightened age, John Couey kidnapped Jessica Lunsford from the safety of her bedroom. She was nine years old. Couey held the child prisoner in his own house and raped her for three days, locking her in a closet while he reported to his regular job. On the third day he bound the little girl's wrists with speaker wire and stuffed her in a garbage bag. Then he buried her alive in a shallow grave, and left her to suffocate beneath the earth.

Horrified lawmakers crafted a law in Jessica's name providing mandatory prison sentences for those who prey on children, and requiring them to be electronically monitored as long as they are alive. "Jessica's Law" is only one of several statutes to save others from such fates that have been named for those who were not saved. There is Megan's Law and there is the Amber Alert, and there is the Adam Walsh Child Protection and Safety Act.

Adam was only six years old when he was taken from the parking lot of a store near his home. Sixteen days later police found Adam's severed head 120 miles from the scene of his abduction. A convicted serial killer confessed to the crime, and described to the police in gruesome detail the sexual torments he inflicted on Adam before beheading him. The killer then taunted Adam's grieving father, offering to sell him information about the location of his son's body parts. The offer was refused, but authorities never filed charges for the crime. They were of the opinion that the killer was merely boasting to enhance his reputation to the similarly inclined.

The law inspired by Adam's death requires criminals who commit sexual crimes to register with authorities and then to update their information at three-month intervals, with failure to register a felony. Yet the law was only passed over the widespread objections of "human rights" advocates who were concerned that the liberties of sexual criminals were being infringed. At the time of its passage, there were half a million sexual criminals in America, and the whereabouts of a hundred thousand of them already identified were unknown.

According to information provided by the National Crime Alert Registry, six out of every ten rape victims are under the age of eighteen, and half of those are not even eleven. The chance that a male child will become the victim of a sex offender is one in six, a girl one in three. The National Center for Victims of Crime informs the interested that the sexual abuse of children is a family affair and more than half of rape victims are kin. This makes attempts to identify and prosecute the criminals difficult and often impossible. It also poses an obstacle that is almost insuperable to the detection of these crimes in the first place. When the bonds of love are set against the claims of justice, how can there be one or the other?

Abuse begets abuse, generation on generation; adult criminals are spawned by the cruelties of their parents, and the misery proceeds through time without end. Subtler forms of torment that families inflict also scar the innocent and prompt the victims to punish strangers in return. Can there be an end to this chain of suffering? Laws against child abuse have been enacted by governments throughout the civilized world, but the tide flows unabated. A hundred years after the Emancipation Proclamation there are tens of millions of children sold into sexual slavery the world over.

But what practical remedy is available? How can we prevent the sins of the parents from being visited on their children? By monitoring all families, abrogating their privacy and individual rights? By the forced removal of children from their homes to raise them under the auspices of the state? And who will monitor the overseers?

The arc of the moral universe is indeed bent, but there is no one and no way to unbend it.

V

In the morning when I prepare for the day ahead and shave the new grown stubble from my cheeks, I often think of my father who has been gone these twenty-five years. The bathroom where he performed these same rituals also served as our family field hospital. I was an avid competitor as a child in neighborhood games and often ran shoeless in the streets, which led to scrapes and cuts requiring attention. Among the comforting memories I can still retrieve are those of my father as our resident medic dressing the wounds I acquired at play. Later I was able to see that he was a weak man, unable to rescue himself from the deeper hurts that life inflicted. But when I was young he was my Gibraltar, and I was confident his strength would never fail me.

Every morning, I would wake up early to watch his preparations, sitting on the closed bowl beside the sink, or standing discreetly to his rear my head rising just above his waist. A towel would be draped around his small athletic frame, which faced the mirror, his bowed calves visible under the towel edge. The routine never varied. He would lather his cheeks and puff them out, first one and then the other, then pull on his chin with his free hand until the surface became taut and smooth. In measured strokes he would draw the razor down from his ear in the same deliberate manner with which he applied the bandages to my wounds. When the foam was swept away, he would tear a tissue into little squares and place them over the spots of blood where the skin had been nicked by the errant blade.

Ever since my angina I have had to be careful about cuts. The blood thinners prescribed by my cardiologist create a moderate hazard when the skin is pierced. A slight break barely noticed before could cause blood to pour like an open faucet. Fortunately, as a result of technical advances over time the disposable razors my father used have been greatly improved. Gone are the single-edge Gillettes whose scratch and tug led to inevitable breaks. My razor now bears the same company name but comes with a track holding five finely spaced blades that vibrate with an electric pulse regulated by a microchip. The shave this complex device provides is so smooth I can hardly feel the hairs being severed as it passes.

This is the detail that provokes the memories. For though my father was normally silent during his morning routine, he would sometimes halt his razor mid-stroke and turn to where I was standing to explain to me the sinister designs of its makers. These were the capitalists, who were in business to make profits and not to serve human needs. Consequently, Gillette would never create a perfect blade, or one that would last longer or even forever. He delivered this homily on many occasions, varying his examples to illustrate the evils of the system he hated, and to demonstrate how its profiteers blocked his hopes for a better life.

Summoned from memory, these sermons became irresistible occasions for my own second thoughts. Whenever a company came to market with a new product, I was inspired to review his long ago claims. One razor manufacturer even produced an "Infinity Blade" to last forever. It hardly mattered whether the promise was fulfilled. The claim reflected a market reality that nullified my father's beliefs. To succeed, capitalists had to develop products that met their customers' needs better than those of their rivals. In other words, what made profit *possible* was the satisfaction of human needs. My father had overlooked so obvious a truth I realized he had never understood the system he was so desperate to overthrow. Each time a product innovation made life better—and for more people than ever in the past—it caused me to think of the wasted devotions of my father's life.

One summer after the fall of Communism, I had occasion to visit the Czech Republic and found myself on a tour of Prague Castle, an imposing edifice overlooking the River Moldau. The Castle had housed the kings of Bohemia since the twelfth century and had been the seat of the Holy Roman Empire after that. But for me it provided a conclusive text confounding my father's faith. Its royal rooms were arched by forty-foot ceilings, and were fitted with the finest furniture and rare tapestries. But these august chambers were lit only by candles, and their cavernous interiors were heated by wood fires, and there were no bathrooms in sight. Water was brought in with buckets, and the only toilets were wooden baskets. It occurred to me that the ordinary home of the poorest worker in the capitalist societies my father hated was richer in human comforts than the most opulent palaces of the kings of old. It was a gift of the very system that continued to oppress the utopian imaginations of progressives everywhere.

VI

We seek to persuade ourselves that the past is more substantial than a dream by speaking of its actors as people who have *made history*, as though an elaborate architecture was in the process of completion. We describe events as "historic," suggesting that a cornerstone has been set in place. But this is a metaphor, and there is no such architecture. One day we will forget the heroes and their stories, and history itself, whose path is not an upward slope as progressives like to think but a cycle of rises and falls, as the Romans long ago understood. Those who triumph in the present will be conquered later, and what is built today will be gone tomorrow, and eventually there will be no one to mourn its passing.

We live inside the historical drama in order to gain the comforts of a religious faith. For unlike the narratives of our individual lives we cannot bring history to a halt. It is a fiction we do not control, and it will roll on without us. The illusion of a historical progress creates meanings for our individual stories, and not even the wisest among us seem able to do without them.

Despite his exceptional insight, even Dostoevsky was unable to live with the idea of history without a purpose. Sometime in his mid-fifties, at the peak of his creative powers, he persuaded himself that history, in fact, was structured like a novel with themes an artist could decipher and become a prophet in the process.

In January 1877 he wrote: "It is evident, that the time is at hand for something eternal, something millenarian, something that has been in preparation in the world since the very beginning of its civilization." He was referring to a conflict now nearly forgotten that was brewing in the Balkans, which were then ruled by the Islamic empire of the Ottoman Turks. Four months after Dostoevsky wrote these words, the Russian Czar declared war on the Ottomans, putting his country at the head of a coalition of Christian nations seeking to liberate themselves from four hundred years of Muslim rule. To Dostoevsky these events appeared as the road to Armageddon since Russia's war might lead to the liberation of Constantinople, which had been the holy seat of the Orthodox Church before the Islamic conquest. In the prophet's imagination a Russian victory would prepare the way for a theological utopia, in which the world would be ruled by an authentic Christian faith.

Earlier, Dostoevsky had written in his notebooks: "I want the full kingdom of Christ." He had then crossed out the words "I want" and put in their place: "I *believe* in the full kingdom of Christ." And then: "I believe that this kingdom will be accomplished, and it will be with us in Russia." Other nations lived only for themselves but Russia was different, he believed; it was a nation that lived for Christ. "Now that the time has come," Russia would take the lead in establishing the kingdom of God, "becoming the servant of all for the sake of universal reconciliation ... [and] ... the ultimate unifying of humanity." He had become his own Inquisitor incarnate.

Dostoevsky knew that the secular world would look with scorn on his vision of a Christian millennium. But he had an answer: his messianic vision mirrored their view of a progressive future. "You believe (and I along with you) in a common humanity—that is, that at some time the natural barriers and prejudices that until now have prevented the free communion of nations through the egoism of national aspirations, will someday fall before the light of reason and consciousness, and that only then will peoples begin to live in a single spirit and in accord as brothers, rationally and lovingly striving for general harmony. Tell me, gentlemen, what can be higher or more sacred than this faith... ?"

What indeed? Dostoevsky remained convinced that this was the faith for which Russia had been chosen. Until the current historical moment, he wrote, Western Civilization had been dominated by two failed attempts to achieve the universal community of man. These were the utopian quests embodied in the Roman Church and secular socialism, which he thought of as different versions of the same promise. Socialism was a totalitarian religion that sought "nothing other than the *compulsory* union of humanity." It owed its provenance to "an idea derived from ancient Rome that was subsequently completely preserved in Catholicism."

In Dostoevsky's view the true Christian idea of individual freedom had been preserved in the Eastern Orthodox Church. Now, under Russia's aegis, "the fulfillment of the destinies of humans on earth" would be achieved voluntarily through a spiritual conversion to this Christian truth. Finally the reconciliation of humanity's warring factions would be achieved through the defeat of Islam and the unification of the Slavic peoples under the Russian *imperium*, in which Christianity was a living creed.

VII

Every quest for a redemption in this life faces a necessary enemy in the opponents of its promised future. So it was with Dostoevsky's quest for a universal harmony in Christ, whose path was blocked by a people who were by nature insular and self-centered, as Dostoevsky viewed them—Jews. "The Yid and his bank are now reigning over everything," he confided to his notebooks, "over Europe, education, civilization, socialism." The Jew "will use [his bank] to uproot Christianity and destroy civilization."

Like every would-be redeemer, Dostoevsky viewed the apocalypse as imminent: "The Jews' ... reign is drawing nigh! Coming soon is the complete triumph of ideas before which feelings of love for humanity, the longing for truth, Christian feelings ... must give way." He regarded Jews as a self-regarding, self-seeking tribe among the nations, who refused to be assimilated to the cultures they inhabited, and thus to the common good.

On the other hand, the same characteristics contributed to the fact that Jews were a people that had outlived every other. "Even the mightiest of the world's civilizations never lasted half of forty centuries," Dostoevsky marveled, yet he also realized that insularity and egoism were an insufficient explanation for this fact. "In order to lose so many times their territory, their political independence, their laws, almost even their religion—to lose these things and each time to unite once more, to be reborn once more," the Jews had to be continually reborn in "their old idea."

This idea was the belief that they were chosen by God, who had given them His covenant, which Dostoevsky described in these words: "Go forth from the other nations, form thine own entity and know that henceforth thou art the only one before God … [and] even when thou art scattered over the face of the earth and among all other peoples—pay no heed; have faith in these things that have been promised unto thee." The promise of redemption had given the Jews the will and strength to be reborn in defeat, and to survive above all others.

There was an unnoticed irony in this rebuke: the same promise was also the self-centered heart of the mission that Dostoevsky had embraced—a Russian salvation of the world. How did this irony escape the artist, whose Inquisitor had identified the need of human beings to worship a God in history who would release them from insecurity and doubt? The torment of their uncertainty was so great, he warned, that "even when gods disappear from the earth; they will fall down before idols just the same"; for the sake of a god to worship, they will make war on each other and will do so "to the end of the world."

VIII

When I have vanished like those before me, my family name will soon be gone with me. Of my four grandchildren, three are females who will probably take the surnames of their husbands, should they marry; the fourth is my daughter's son who bears the surname of his father. But this eclipse will mean little. In our family the name "Horowitz" is hardly three generations old, having been invented for my grandfather by immigration officials at Ellis Island when he came to America in 1905. Who knows who we were before that?

About our family prior to their arrival in America, I know very little, which probably reflects my father's discomfort with the past. He was incurious enough about his lineage that he never seems to have inquired about the actual name of his own father in the country of his birth. "Gurevitch or Gurevoy" was all he said to me.

He also had a particular disliking for the relatives on my mother's side, whose men were more successful than he. Consequently, our contacts were rare, and I had little of their family history imparted to me as a child. My mother went along with this prejudice, perhaps choosing it as a path less stressful than resistance. As a result, all the knowledge I have of the lives that preceded me is a thin line of memories beginning with my mother's father, whose name was Shmuel Braunstein or Bronstein, I have no idea which.

Shmuel was a Rumanian Jew who emigrated to America before the turn of the last century and was one of eight wine-making brothers who left Rumania because they had been forbidden as Jews to own land or cultivate a vineyard. In America they became merchants, owning dry goods stores in New Haven and New York. They shed their family name, half of them deciding to call themselves "Brown" and the other half "Stone." In this American transition my grandfather Shmuel Braunstein became "Sam Brown."

I must have met my great uncles as a youngster but I have no memory of them. Like most of the details of my grandfather's life, I do not know the dates of his passage to America. But sometime after his arrival, he married Rose Abramovitz (or Abramovich), a young girl of eighteen who had been born on these shores. I know the year they were married, which was 1898, because it is stamped on some serving pieces made of blue glass, which my grandmother received as a wedding gift and handed down to my mother, who left them for me. About her family I know nothing except that they arrived with the first great immigration waves after the Civil War. Rose and Sam had two children whom they called "Blanche" and "Harold," names, as my mother observed, that were somewhat bland and hardly Jewish.

My uncle Harold was a talented musician who studied with the composers Leonard Bernstein and Aaron Copland, and was a man of strong and often inflexible views when it came to defending the integrity of his art. Consequently, although he lived for seventy years, his works were never played or recorded, and he failed to receive the recognition he deserved.

In his forties, he taught at the High School of Music and Art, where he created the Renaissance Chorus, which was devoted to the era that was closest to his heart. After his death, his students kept the chorus together but met at infrequent intervals. When they were themselves in their sixties and seventies, the chorus members organized a concert of his works on a weekend that would have been his 100th birthday if he had lived so long.

I went to New York to attend his centennial, which was held in the Advent Lutheran Church on the Upper East Side, and there I heard his music for the first time. The organizers provided concert notes, which contained an excerpt from the diary of the composer Ned Rorem, who was one of his students, and which offered this observation: "If forty years later he died unknown while ever superior to many an interferer, some of us feel that in his surly urge to avoid the reeking herd—in his not playing the game which is part of the rat race—he sailed above the storm but, unlike the Eagle of the Rock, he sailed quite out of sight."

This could also be said of the entire family of Braunsteins and Horowitzes. One day it will be true of me as well.

IX

We can look back thousands of years through the images left by those who went before us and still see ourselves in them. Their thoughts and hopes, emotions and disappointments, are all familiar. But in one respect a gulf has opened between us that cannot be bridged. Scientific advances have progressed to a degree that has made our own lives unimaginable to our ancestors. A result of these advances is that it is now possible for a Jew to trace his lineage through a single gene sample back to the time of Aaron and Moses.

The opportunity this provides is a consequence of the inbreeding of our forebears, and also the isolation imposed by our sense of entitlement, and our persecution by those who resent us for it. On the other hand, as Jews we do not need genetic markers to determine our identity, since our history is itself a genome. Consider that two millennia after our dispersal by the Romans, the Horowitzes and Braunsteins were still on the run; they had left a hostile country for a strange new one; and they were still pursuing the promised land.

When I consider how my life and the life of the Jews have been shaped by these facts, I cannot help but wonder about the illusions that possessed our forebears to take on the most powerful empire the world had ever seen. As it happens this question arose at the time of their rebellion, and was recorded for posterity by Yosef ben

Matityahu, one of the Jewish generals who defended
Jerusalem against the Roman advance.

In the course of the siege, Yosef was captured by the
Romans and became their historian and also their coun-
selor. He changed his name to "Flavius Josephus" and
under this Latin pseudonym wrote a seven-volume
account of the conflict called *The Jewish War*. In his history, Josephus put the argument against the rebellion into
the mouth of a Jewish leader who sought to dissuade
others from their fateful campaign: "What confidence is
it that elevates you to oppose the Romans? Are you richer
than the Gauls, stronger than the Germans, wiser than
the Greeks, more numerous than all men upon the hab-
itable earth? ... You are the only people who think it a
disgrace to be servants to those to whom all the world
has submitted...."

Josephus understood the passion of his people, which
was to submit to no God but their own. It was the covenant that promised their salvation. But the Romans also
knew that a common worship secured a common rule,
and they required subjects to bow to the gods who sus-
tained their empire. Eventually, Rome's emperors

declared *themselves* to be gods, and demanded a religious adoration from their subject peoples. When they attempted to place their statues inside the Temple in Jerusalem, the Jews rebelled, and responded, "No king but God," for "God is to be [our] only ruler and lord."

X

Five centuries after the Romans drove the Jews out of Judea and Samaria, the land their God had promised was conquered by Islamic armies and brought under Muslim rule. The Muslims built a mosque over the ruins of Solomon's Temple, and made Jews across their empire a subject people. Centuries later, the Muslim empire was defeated in World War I. The European victors divided up the ruins granting the descendants of the Jews three slivers of desert land to create a Jewish state. After nearly two millennia they had finally come home.

But Islam's prophet had cursed the Jews, warning his followers the day of redemption would only come "when the Muslims fight the Jews and kill them, when the Jews hide behind the rocks and the trees, and the rocks and the trees cry out: 'O Muslim, there is a Jew hiding behind me. Come and kill him.'" As Muslim fortunes revived, the war against the Jews began again.

Atheists attribute the hostility that has followed us through the ages to theology—a hatred that emanates from rival religions. This is true of the war between Muslims and Jews, but in what god did Hitler put his trust?

Jew hatred also exists in countries without us, like Malaysia and Japan, and Poland after its Jewish population was destroyed. As one writer observed, it is a venom that is in some ways absolutely unique. "Sinhalese who don't like Tamils or Hutu who regard Tutsi as 'cockroaches,' do not accuse their despised neighbors of harboring a plan—or of possessing the ability—to bring off a secret world government based on the occult control of finance." Belief in the conspiracy of the Jews is the heart of an atheistic faith. It puts a comforting order into the world, and feeds the illusion that a salvation awaits, if the devil can be removed.

XI

At seventy-one years, I have lived longer than both Marcus Aurelius and Dostoevsky, and indeed most of the people who preceded me on this earth. The ability to extend our lives is one of the gifts of science that encourages us to believe that things are getting better, and to this extent they may be. But the same advances have enabled us to monitor each other more closely, constricting our freedoms, and to kill each other more easily and on a far greater scale than ever before. It has also brought the warring sides of humanity into closer proximity, making no place safe.

Here is a Jewish perspective: it is three millennia since Moses led us to the border of the promised land, which was situated on the west bank of the Jordan, which Muslims now rule. It is almost two thousand years since the Romans expelled us from this very territory, Judea and Samaria, and renamed it "Palestine." This is time enough to review our progress and weigh the balance, which is this: wherever we have migrated in our exile to make our homes we have built thriving and creative cultures, yet we are still among the most hated and hunted people on earth, and the only ones who have been chosen for this role the world over.

*He who has seen present things has seen all, both
everything that has taken place from all eternity
and everything that will be for time without
end …*

Deep in the millennial past, Jews were the original
progressives and invented the idea that we are on our
way towards a brighter future, which perhaps is why our
history is so filled with tragedy and defeat. We have survived so long now and are spread so far and wide as to
provide a measure for those who can handle it, of where
we are going and where history is actually headed, which
is nowhere.

XII

Several times a week now, I take a walk alone to the
end of the long and leafless driveway in front of my house
in the Santa Maria Valley. I walk past the avocado grove
on my neighbor's side and onto the street where I turn
the corner, which is lined with hedges, and go out the
community gate. Once beyond the perimeter, I follow

the horse path up the hill until I can see the valley floor below me. There is an agricultural plain in the crease between the mountains that has been planted with a fresh crop, and the hillsides are green again from the recent rains.

If I push myself too hard on the upward slope my chest begins to tighten, and I am reminded of what I have come through and where I am headed. If the pain is too strong, I stop to rest before making the turn to come alongside the pastures and pipe corrals where the Warm-bloods loiter with their colts in the shade. Then I make my way down the hill to complete the circle and return home.

Unlike my walks in Calabasas or the shorter outings I take within the gated community, I do not bring the dogs with me. Winnie's joints have become too sore for such strenuous exercises, and while the little dogs are still limber enough to make the walk, there is no way the big dog would understand why we had left her. So I leave them all behind.

Sometimes I stop to look down at the valley below and reflect on its ghosts. The Chumash Indians lived in these environs before the Europeans came, and probably before the times of Moses and Christ. Their stay ended when the *Californios* crossed over from Mexico and Spain, carrying diseases against which the native inhabitants had no defenses. The Hispanics took their brief turn, and were then replaced by the English-speaking conquerors who preserved the names of their *ranchos*, which still mark the landscape and are occupied by people like me. And who will come when we are gone?

Despite all that I think I know, I still return to the security of my stories, and am content to live in their worlds. And what is the alternative? Without our stories our lives would be chaos and our existence unbearable. Therefore, I keep moving forward, as I always have, though my steps have slowed and my passions are dimmed. My time is spent reflecting on these facts, and carrying on the work that has taken me this far, looking out for family, friends, and animals as I go. Beyond these personal obligations I have concerns for my country and for the perils of the Jews because their fates cannot be separated from mine. Most of all, I try to be a support to my wife and do what I can for my children and their children, who are quite independent of me now and have lives that go on without me. I am impelled forward by my writing, and that is the reason for doing it. Although there is always a feeling of loss at the close of a book, I am content to be coming to the end of this one, and look forward to its publication, even though few people will read it, and then there will be none.

I do not dwell on thoughts of oblivion but refer to the advice of the Roman, using my knowledge of the future to muffle the distress of the present. Sometimes I take a sentimental turn and imagine that when it is my time to go I will be joining my daughter Sarah and, along with her, my parents, and also the members of our family known and unknown who went before me down the ages to the beginning of time.

Some days I sit on my back porch looking up through the trees and their shivering boughs to the sky above, and think about going, and find myself completely at peace with this prospect. I have felt this way for some time now, comfortable with the idea that soon I will be no one and nowhere, and comforted in a stoic way by the knowledge that it doesn't add up. Perhaps my daughter's passing helped me to arrive at this peace. In any case, the loss ahead of me is no different from any along the way, except that there will be no pain.

We are wounded by losses and rage to have them reversed. But eventually we come to terms with our fate, knowing that this was all there was ever going to be.

In the year gone by, I fulfilled an obligation to my daughter by putting together a book of the writings she left behind, which occupied so much of her short time on this earth. My children built a library for her among the Abayudayah, a tribe of African Jews in Uganda, whom she served and to whom we have sent a package of her books. And that, in the end, is what my father left me, too, and what each of us leaves to our children: a bookshelf and a death.

Because of his interest in creating a new world, my father generally lacked interest in the improvements to this one that did not hasten its coming. His grandchildren have been freed from this illusion and understand that the life we have now is all we will get, and therefore is what is important. My sons and daughters have worked to bring health and pleasure to others and to aid troubled and disabled children. They understand that if the world is to be redeemed it will be one individual at a time. I take satisfaction in that.

At some point in every day, I return to my writing. It is not that this work is important to anyone, though long ago I acquired an audience to whom it may seem so; and perhaps there has been some good that has come through my words. I do this work because it is important to me.

Often I play music in the background when I write, and sometimes it is the *Requiem Mass* that Mozart wrote in his thirty-fifth year for an anonymous stranger. It was the last piece he ever composed. While he was working on the *Requiem* he was stricken with an illness so severe that he told his wife he was writing it for himself. His intuition was correct, and he died some days later before he was able to finish a piece that has been played by millions through the centuries since. The only parts of the *Requiem* he was able to complete before taking his last breath were the Introit or "entrance" (*Grant them eternal rest, Lord, and let perpetual light shine on them*) and the Kyrie (*Lord, have mercy on us*). He left behind him sketches of the rest, and was still writing on the last day he was alive.

AUTHOR'S NOTE

I wish to thank my wife April for bringing our animals—Jake, Lucy, Winnie, Alvin, and Diddy, and our
new additions, Coco and Lucky—into our family, and
for her friendship and big-hearted approach to life, which
have been the greatest gifts to mine.

I wish to thank my children, Jonathan, Benjamin, and
Anne, and my stepson Jon, for being creative and compassionate individuals and loving offspring, and I wish
to thank their children, Julia, Mariah, Sophie, and Elvis,
for being the same.

I am in debt to my friend Mike Finch for his support,
which has been indispensable in carrying out my work

and moving forward. In ways more than he knows, he has made this book possible.

I am grateful to my closest friend Peter Collier, for reading the work in manuscript and making critical suggestions at the outset; and to my publishers, Jeff Carneal and Marji Ross for their faith in me and support for my work; and to my editors Farahn Morgan and Mary Beth Baker for looking after my text.

The following works by other authors were particularly helpful in composing this one: Joseph Frank, *Dostoevsky*, 5 volumes; Gary Saul Morson, *Boundaries of Genre: Dostoevsky's Diary of a Writer and the Traditions of Literary Utopia*; James P. Scanlan, *Dostoevsky the Thinker*; David I. Goldstein, *Dostoevsky and the Jews*; and Flavius Josephus, *The Jewish War*.